WORKING DADS AND BALANCING ACTS

THE SECRET TO MAKING IT WORK

SARAH MACONACHIE

KMD
BOOKS

Edited by Hannah Lawrence
Interior design by Dylan Ingram
Proofread by Gill Hunter
Cover design by Dylan Ingram

National Library of Australia Catalogue-in-Publication data:
Working Dads and Balancing Acts/Sarah Maconachie

ISBN:
978-0-9924628-0-2
(Hardback)

ISBN:
978-0-9924628-7-1
(Paperback)

ISBN:
978-0-9924628-9-5
(Ebook)

DEDICATION

To all the incredible dads out there, this is for you. To those who have wanted a family their entire life, and those who never really thought about it. To the dads who feel strongly about being the 'provider,' working tirelessly to make ends meet and support their family, sacrificing family time while doing so. And to the dads who have challenged societal norms, either staying at home with their children or going part-time to take on the parenting responsibilities while their partner goes to work. To those dads who felt prepared and those who didn't know what the F**K they were in for—this book is for all of you.

There are dads in this book who have had difficult upbringings, making them determined to create a different life for their own children. There are dads who have their own fathers as incredible role models, helping shape the expectations of what being a good dad means. There are dads who have asked for flexible work arrangements and been told "no," and others who left their jobs to find the flexibility they wanted. We hear from leaders and CEOs who are paving the way for gender equality and parental justice in the workplace—something we are all thankful for.

To the dads out there who are looking for guidance from other dads, to the dads who are looking to be better partners and fathers, to the bosses and workplaces who don't understand why flexibility for fathers is important—I hope this book inspires you.

To all the dads who have participated in sharing their journey in this book, and to those who read these pages reflecting on their own journey—I thank you.

Sarah :)

CONTENTS

ACKNOWLEDGE
MEET THE AUTHORS

PETER CLARK
ONSTRUCTION SERVICES & IN-
FRASTRUCTURE PTY LTD | TRIBELY
| FOURTH SUN | SURFING THE
SPECTRUM

ADRIAN ENGEL
THE FATHERING PROJECT

DAVID TAYLOR
POLICE OFFICER

JASON FRISHMAN
JOURNEY MEN | CONNECTED
FATHERS

ACKNOWLEDGE
MEET THE AUTHORS

BRADLEY RAYNOR
COGNITO

CHARLIE MAUGHAN
IMAGESEVEN

RHYS MACONACHIE
WESTPAC

PETER BENNETT
CEO CLOUGH

ACKNOWLEDGE
MEET THE AUTHORS

CHRIS LLOYD
MANAGER/CONSULTANT

DR. ROBERT SCOTT
GP, PI AND UNI SC AND NON-EX-
ECUTIVE DIRECTOR OF LEA

GEORGE ROLOGAS
THE BRAND SOCIETE

JOHN PARK
PARTNER DENTONS

ACKNOWLEDGE

MEET THE AUTHORS

THOMAS BATCHELOR
SHELL ENERGY

DOUGLAS VEAL
AUSTRALIAN PUBLIC SERVICE

ROLFE PIKE
PAMWE GROUP

ROWYN BARTLETT
WESTERN POWER

ACKNOWLEDGE

MEET THE AUTHORS

BARRY MONE
CHARLIE'S HOPE

SAM HILL
COFFEY TESTING

STAN ROLFE
KEYWORDS STUDIOS AUSTRALIA

JOE BOVELL
ECO GROWTH

INTRODUCTION

W
e are here to acknowledge the incredible role that dads play in their children's lives. Society is rapidly changing, and the involvement of fathers is becoming more and more prevalent. In the generations before, the role of a dad was to just provide. In decades of movies, we see fathers portrayed as the hunter and gatherer, coming home after a long hard day's work to a lovely home-cooked meal, being greeted at the door by his children's big smiles and a gorgeous wife with a stiff drink ready and fresh bread in the oven.

Dads play an incredible role in the upbringing of children. As a society, we are really starting to understand that the role of fathers is just as important as that of mothers, and this book is a celebration of parental stereotypes slowly fading.

Upon these pages, you'll read raw, honest stories from fathers from all walks of life. Their words will make you think, make you feel happy, sad, heartbroken, proud, and inspired all at once.

When paternity leave wasn't an option, there are dads who have become advocates. When father's groups were non-existent, there are dads who have created their own. When stay-at-home fathers were judged by their peers, there are dads who wore the badge proudly. When mental health challenges prevailed, there are dads who have sought help to become a better father, partner, man.

This book is a call to action for dads to create the life they love, to find the flexibility they desire, to speak up for what they need, and to have the courage to seek the work/life balance required for them and their family.

At the end of this book, you'll find thought-provoking worksheets that will challenge where you're at now, where you want to go, and who you want to be. Let this book take you on a journey of self-discovery and empowerment. You have the ability to create a life that you have complete control over.

A father's presence is such a gift to children.

PETER CLARK

"

THESE ARE THE GOLDEN YEARS,
FILLED WITH EVERLASTING
MEMORIES, LAUGHS, AND TEARS.
THE EARLY YEARS ARE THE PUREST
AND RAWEST AS A PARENT.

"

Peter, husband to his high school sweetheart Jess, is a father to two daughters, Indiana (Indy) and Tilly, currently aged four and two, respectively. Jess, with a background in early childhood teaching, inspired Peter to embark on years of study and research into children, taking a pedagogy approach. While Peter's learning journey included reading books on parenting, he discovered that no amount of reading equated to navigating through the intensely incredible experience of being a dad. Peter also credits his learning to the collective wisdom of all the parents he has connected with over the years, regardless of the different stages of their parenting journey.

PETER CLARK

AUTHOR NAME: PETER CLARK
BUSINESS NAME: CONSTRUCTION SERVICES & INFRASTRUC-
TURE PTY LTD | TRIBELY | FOURTH SUN | SURFING THE SPECTRUM
POSITION: OWNER
BUSINESS INDUSTRY: ENGINEERING | BUSINESS SERVICES |
MANAGEMENT CONSULTING | NFP
WEBSITE: CSIGROUP.SERVICES | FOURTHSUN.COM.AU | SURF-
INGTHESPECTRUM.ORG
LINKEDIN: LINKEDIN.COM/IN/PETECLARKY

Being a dad is the most underpaid, undervalued, and over-important role in the world (apart from being a mum, of course). You're like the engine of a car. The driver doesn't really stop to think about you all that often, but just expects you to keep turning over and to keep on going. Even though your kids won't say it directly to your face all that often, their actions and feelings towards you will tell the story. You are Superman. With a cape. To them, you can fly. You can lift the world up in one hand. You inspire them, drive them forward, make them laugh. They listen to you. They watch you. They want to be like you and copy the things that you do.

I had what I call a '70s upbringing in the '90s. I am the middle child of three boys, and I was very lucky to grow up in Sydney, Australia. The house we lived in for the majority of my childhood was in a cul-de-sac where everybody knew each other. There were about 10 or so other kids in the street, and we would all hang out whenever we could. The rules were simple; come home for dinner when the streetlights come on and don't get hurt or into any trouble. Luckily, Mum rarely saw us 'bombing it' down the steep street on roller blades or a skateboard, seeing how fast we could go before bailing onto someone's front lawn. Whoever got the furthest down the street before the end of the cul-de-sac won.

My mum was a stay-at-home mum and did an incredible job raising us three boys. The logistics behind keeping us fed was a full-time job, let alone the constant stain removal required from grass or mud on our clothes. Mum worked before having kids, and reluctantly gave it up to take care of us while Dad worked full-time. Daycare wasn't an option back then, so this was the most common family dynamic. Dad has always been an entrepreneur and self-employed. He did a tough electrician apprenticeship on the railways, and then put himself through engineering school at night to become an electrical engineer, all whilest working full-time in his own electrical contracting business. He was commuting almost two hours each way to his job at Brighton Le Sands and then TAFE at Granville at night, and then back to the central coast. This was all while my older brother John was a baby.

Both parents were (and still are) incredibly committed to us and gave parenting their all. Dad learnt from his dad, believing the best way that you can contribute as a father to your family is financial security. Dad wasn't home often due to his long hours working for his business, but when he was, he was 100% ours. We were always doing physical activity, whether it was swimming at the beach, learning how to surf, or taking us on long bike rides to tire us out. When reflecting on my childhood and my parent's parenting style, it conjures up one word in my mind: reliable. I can depend on my parents. It's not sexy and it's not flashy parenting. But it is foundational to everything else.

My wife, Jess, and I struggled to fall pregnant. We knew we wanted to be parents quite young, and once we discovered that we were facing a fertility battle, we started the process. Through many blood samples, scans, doctors, referrals to specialists and appointments, we finally found a process that worked. After three rounds of IVF injections, we discovered that we were pregnant with a girl.

Jess went into labour at 2.30am on 13th April 2019. We lived over an hour from the hospital and were reasonably casual about the start of contractions. A couple of hours into the labour, I timed the contractions again and realised that they were less than five minutes apart. A call to the hospital and they shouted at us to get there as soon as possible. We jumped into the car and realised that I had hardly any petrol left! My one job. I had to decide whether I was going to confess my shortcomings or risk it straight to the hospital. I played it safe and pulled into a service station. It was probably the fastest refuelling that service station has ever seen. Flying down the motorway, our baby was trying to come out in the car! We only just made it, and Indiana was born 15-minutes after we arrived at the hospital.

I took three weeks paternity leave with Indy. I would've taken more if I could. These truly are the most precious days and weeks as you're discovering everything for the first time! My advice during this time would be to take the leave you can afford. If you have to go back to work for financial reasons, take what you can in the initial block (e.g., 2-3 weeks), and then take a day or two a week for a longer period of time to spread it out. We were living an hour and a half out of Sydney and away from family, so whatever I could do to help made a big difference for Jess.

In that first six weeks, we found a dad rhythm that worked really well with going back to work. Jess would be with Indy from waking up until I got home from work. I negotiated with my work to arrive at 7:00am and leave at 3:00pm. This meant that I could get up and leave for my big commute while Jess and Indy were still asleep (hopefully) and be back earlier to spend as much time as possible with them. I would do Indy's bath and read books to her and sing to her before putting her to bed at around 6.30pm. When she would inevitably wake, say 10:00pm or 11:00pm, I would give her a bottle and a cuddle and put her back to bed. This gave Jess the break she needed as well as my one-on-one time with Indy. Some nights I fell asleep with her in my arms on the lounge from the night feed. Weekends were spent as a family hanging out altogether – we loved going for a walk or going to the beach.

I'm an accountant for a small engineering business. I worked full-time in the office up until COVID-19, but now I only work 2-3 day in the office a week. This suits my ability to balance being a parent and working perfectly. I spend a lot of time with the kids and shift my work around to suit the needs of my family first. As long as I am getting my work done and on time, then there are no problems from my work's end. For example, Indy and Tilly do swimming lessons on a Monday. I did all of their swimming lessons when they were younger, and now I share it with my wife. Usually, we'll do alternate weeks. So, for that hour or so time slot in my workday, I block out 10.30am to 12:00pm on Microsoft Teams so that the people I work with know that I am busy.

Any fork in the road type of decisions that has to be made between my work or my family, I always put my family first. I've learnt from my own dad's mistakes and lessons; that the most precious and finite resource you can give your kids is time. It's the only thing that cannot be copied, cannot be replaced, and cannot be outsourced. It's the only time where the typical adage of 'quality not quantity' is inverted. While quality time is incredibly import-ant, I would argue that the quantity of time is more important.

My wife has shifted from her previous job as an early childhood teacher to now bookkeeping remotely. She does it for a few small clients, and the flexibility means that the kids don't have to go to daycare. When you crunch the numbers, working more to pay for more daycare is often a net zero transaction.

Although it can feel overwhelming at times, with many occa-sions when I need to step out the back door for deep breaths by myself, I am now harvesting the fruits from the seeds of so much time and proximity with my two daughters. We are extremely close as a family unit and genuinely enjoy spending a significant amount of time together. This has led us to make a big decision: we're heading around Australia in a caravan for more than a year, starting at the end of 2023. To many of our parenting peers we've spoken to, this is their version of a worst nightmare—unlimited time with their kids in a confined space! We couldn't think of anything better.

From those early years and time spent with Indy, we are extremely close. We talk almost every night on her pillow about life and the world and the universe. I'm always asking her to think of big questions to ask me, and we explore the answers together. We have a lot of fun together too, and I make sure that I keep an element of 'being a kid' with her. It can be tempting to lob the weight of the world in expectations and extracurricular activities on our kids. We can want them to grow up even quicker, so that we can reach that illusive 'parenting paradise' mirage that we think we will get to one day. The reality is that the 'mirage' that you see up ahead, is just that—a mirage. It doesn't exist – you need to make the most of your time with your kids as a parent right now. From the very beginning.

My relationship with Tilly keeps reminding me of how much fun parenting can be. It also highlights the differences in development, even between a two-year-old and a four-year-old. The other day, I took both kids for separate bike rides but along the same route. Indy was talking the whole time, asking questions about things we were seeing and about the world around us. Tilly, on the other hand, was singing throughout, pointing out things she could see and now verbalise.

The truth is, you're in the parenting mirage right now. These are the golden years, filled with everlasting memories, laughs, and tears. The early years are the purest and rawest as a parent. The time before they go to school is when you'll be closest to your kids.

Over time, this closeness will decrease slightly and incrementally until you're shocked to find them ready to move out as adults. From the parents I've spoken to over the years, this moment hits them square in the heart because it sneaks up on you. Life is both tedious and brief. The days are long, but the years pass quickly.

I don't have many regrets from my parenting journey thus far. I attribute this to the sheer amount of learning, researching, and asking curious questions to parents I know and respect already. You can ask parents questions that are a year or two ahead of where you are. Or you can ask older people who now have grandkids or great-grandkids. The different perspectives and experiences all coalesce to form your own perspective of what it means to be a parent.

The one thing I would do differently is put less pressure on myself in the early days with Indy. This pressure eases naturally with your second child onwards. It's more of a reality than an intention. Your time and attention is now divided and you'll never spend as much time and energy with your second child onwards as you did with your first. I read so many parenting books before Indy was born. I was trying to be diligent and learn as much as possible. It's like reading a book on how to build a house. You can read that book all you want, but until you pick up the tools and start building, you'll never know what it's actually like. No amount of pre-reading or courses or YouTube how-to videos will prepare you for parenting and how you will react and adapt to the challenge. Why? Because parenting isn't the Instagram story of a perfect picnic at the beach with your family. That's just the tip of the iceberg you want the rest of the world to see. The reality is a war of attrition, every moment of every day. You could be patient with your kids 99% of the time, but that remaining 1%, you might crack. You could do everything within your power to raise and grow incredible human beings, only to feel let down when it seems like it isn't happening.

The best thing you can do as a dad is to be there. Just be there.

Be present. Put the phone away. Remove thoughts of the real world and problems at work. Stop for a moment. Take a deep breath. Look into your child's eyes. Look deeper. Talk to them. Stop. Listen. Ask them a question. Ask more questions. And listen to the actual words that come out of their mouth. Connect with them. Play with them. Laugh with them.

A great lesson I've learned is that we're all on a small rock, floating through space, in a small solar system surrounded by stars and other galaxies. Look up at the sky at night. Understanding space gives us insight into Earth. By gazing at the stars, we can reflect on ourselves through a renewed lens. Our problems become small, our anxieties insignificant, and our focus on enjoying a relatively short life replenished. It makes the meeting you might have missed, or the work call you didn't answer while you were with your kids, seem trivial.

Most workplaces will not put you first. You will not be at the top of their priorities list. When times are tough, they won't be loyal to you. If the numbers don't stack up, you will be let go. They will move on. Within your family, and with your kids, you will be put first. You will be at the top of their list of priorities. When times are tough, they will be loyal to you. There are no numbers to stack up. You will never be let go. They will never move on from you.

When you reach a decision point, when you're asked if you can attend a preschool orientation, a dance concert, or just go to the park on an ordinary Tuesday afternoon, say yes. Say yes to your family. Say yes to your kids. Say yes to endless memories. Say yes to more connections. Say yes to the silly game. Say yes to hopping in the bath with them. Say yes to building the cubby house with blankets again for the fifth time today. Say yes to as much time with them as possible.

One day, when you're older, or even when you're gone, your kids will reflect on their childhood. When someone asks them,

"Was he a good dad?" They'll say yes. Just like you did all those times for them.

ADRIAN ENGEL

> THE STRESS AND THE PRESSURE OF WORKING IN TODAY'S WORLD IS ENORMOUS, AND I DON'T THINK THERE IS A PERFECT FORMULA TO BALANCE BOTH WORK AND A PERSONAL LIFE. AS NEW-AGE PARENTS, WE PUT OURSELVES UNDER SO MUCH PRESSURE TO SUCCEED AT PARENTING, AND WE OFTEN FEEL THAT OUR BEST IS NEVER GOOD ENOUGH.

Adrian, originally from South Africa, moved to Australia in 2016 with his wife and eldest daughter, Allayna. Their second daughter, Kayla, was later born in Australia. While he noticed his wife building friendship circles with other mums at his daughters' school, he found quite the contrary when meeting other dads. After a chance meeting with another dad in the playground, Adrian decided to start a dad's group at the school to provide a space where dads could connect, share experiences, and build new friendships. Due to its success, Adrian partnered with The Fathering Project and implemented its programs within his dad's group at the school. After five years of volunteering for The Fathering Project, Adrian left his original career, in which he spent 22 years in sales and people management, and joined The Fathering Project as the WA State Partnerships and Stakeholder Manager.

ADRIAN ENGEL

AUTHOR NAME: ADRIAN ENGEL
BUSINESS NAME: THE FATHERING PROJECT
POSITION: STATE PARTNERSHIP AND STAKEHOLDER MANAGER
BUSINESS INDUSTRY: NOT FOR PROFIT
LINKEDIN: LINKEDIN.COM/IN/ADRIANENGEL

I had a wonderful childhood filled with some amazing memories. As a young boy, I had to grow up fast and become a responsible big brother to my younger sister. My mother was diagnosed with cancer when I was just seven years old and my sister was two years old. I still remember the day my parents came home and shared the news with us. It was really the first time I ever saw my dad cry. The year was 1988, and the doctors gave my mother six months to live. She passed away in 2003. She lived her life to the fullest and taught us to do the same. She also taught us to be mindful of the way we all treat other people—you just never know what they are going through.

My parents both worked, and I had the privilege of my grandmother raising me for most of my early primary school life. She definitely instilled many of the values that I share with my girls today and I will always be grateful for this. My mother worked up until I was about midway through primary school. Thinking back now, I really enjoyed the opportunities I had when I was able to accompany her to work, and have a clear memory of how many of her lifelong friends started out as her colleagues.

My father on the other hand was someone who had much more of a professional outlook and approach to his career. He was more of an influence on my mindset and the way I approached work and, inevitably, my career. My father left for work at 6:00am and would return no earlier than 5:00pm. I think my dad was very focused and motivated with his work because he didn't have the support from his dad about the career he chose, and possibly felt like he had something to prove, but it was something he never spoke about.

He had a really demanding job, which was filled with many highlights: he worked with my grandfather (my mother's dad) and became his superior, he was the first supervisor of colour at a previously white-only facility, and being a man of colour, this was a major achievement. Not only did my dad work full-time, but throughout most of his career he was studying. After marrying my mum, he completed his first degree, and later on, he earned his master's degree in forensic psychiatry. When I reflect on my dad's career, his academic achievements, and his commitment and dedication, I believe this is what laid the foundation of how I wanted to set myself up with my own career. He was certainly a make-it-work-at-all-costs kind of man. And I have so much respect for him.

When my wife was 35 weeks pregnant, one of her colleagues called me to tell me that my wife's nose was bleeding uncontrollably. By the time we arrived at the doctors, my wife's blood pressure was sky high, and she was immediately admitted to hospital. She was only a month away from delivery, and as you can imagine, we were stressed! The following day we were told that she would have to give birth that week. The doctor said to us, "We are going to have to go and fetch her," and I remember sitting there in just total shock, with this overwhelming feeling, and the only thing I could reply with was, "Fetch who..?" Oh right, it was time for our daughter to be born! On the day of the birth, my wife was in labour the entire day. I remember my sole purpose that day was to be there for her and remain calm throughout the birth despite it being a difficult birth with so much going on. From that moment on our lives changed completely.

I took paternity leave after the birth of my first daughter. At that time, I held the position of senior business unit manager and was one of the youngest in the organisation. I faced pressure not only because many doubted my ability, but also because the unit was not performing well. The timing was not ideal. Work was challenging, and we had just moved into our new family home a couple of weeks before, still in the process of unpacking. I only took one week's leave and, looking back, I wish I took more.

The moment I got back to work, I walked into all that workplace noise. The rat race seemed more evident than ever. There were some difficult and dark days; I remember sleeping in our guest bedroom for a bit so I could leave for work early. I felt so guilty when I spoke to my wife during the day, especially when she expressed how she was struggling. My wife initially took six months maternity leave, and then was approached by her line manager to come back to work a month earlier. We both come from a very strong work ethic upbringing, so she agreed, and my daughter went to a day mother—which is similar to a crèche service—from the age of only five months.

I have actually never told anyone this story, but I feel the need to share it now: One day, after my wife went to work, I was bathing my daughter just like I had 1,000 times before. I placed her on the bed so I could get her ready, just as I had done before. I turned around to get something from her room quickly, I must have been gone for less than half a minute when I heard this massive bump followed by a screaming cry. I went back into our room and found my first born lying on the floor screaming – she had somehow fallen off the bed. I was so distraught and unaware of what to do I immediately called my wife pleading with her to come home and excuse herself from work. All I could think about was that I had dropped our child and had somehow broken her.

I was ready to take her to the hospital. By the time my wife got home, my daughter was fine, it was like nothing had happened. This was not one of my finest dad moments.

In my previous job sector, they did not allow flexible working arrangements. So, when we had Allayna, it was exceptionally difficult for me to find the balance between work and family life. I found myself in a position again where I had just recently been promoted to a state manager level with a completely new team in the organisation that I was working in. I had this feeling to impress everyone. I had the overwhelming desire to convince people that I was competent to be in the position that I was given and consequently sacrificed a lot of family time in order to achieve those objectives. I worked Friday nights after Allayna went to sleep, on Saturday mornings, and even on Sunday afternoons just to keep up and exceed expectations as I felt it was necessary at the time. Unfortunately, I didn't realise the impact this was having on my relationship with my wife.

One day, as I sat around that senior management table, I found that most people weren't in a similar situation that I was, me being a new dad. I felt judged, and there were so many times that I felt I didn't belong there. What was important to me, and things I felt were a priority in my life, were not the same as theirs. It was isolating.

When Allayna was two years old, all I wanted to do was spend as much time as I possibly could with her and at least have some experiences watching her grow up. But I also knew that it was important for me to work hard so that I could provide for her and possibly find myself in a better position a few years down the line so that I would have the luxury and time to spend with my family. This internal conflict is something I believe many men in similar situations grapple with.

To give you some more context about the relationship I had with work and my eldest daughter, by the time she had turned five, I had missed three of her birthdays due to work travel.

Because I was working a lot and sacrificed spending time with Allayna, I made the conscious decision to get her involved in sport quite early on – at the age of four years old. I wanted to make up for lost time. We tried different sports and games, and eventually landed on golf. I used this as a platform to engage with her on a different level. It gave us an opportunity to spend time together and find something that we were both interested in. It has given us so much time together and so much to talk about, making so many unforgettable memories that we will always be able to celebrate together. I am aware, however, that my love for her should not be measured by her achievements, but by the fact that she goes out every weekend and gives it her best and continues to enjoy it. It makes me very proud.

My second daughter, Kayla, was born in 2018 and at the time we were only living in Australia for three years, so, as you can imagine, I was still finding my feet. When Kayla was born, I thought I would have learnt the lessons from balancing work and family life. I hate to say it, but I did not. Work had become even more stressful. I had the pressure of constantly needing to perform and felt again obligated to work even harder to provide for my growing family. I was very fortunate to be able to financially support my wife which allowed her to be a stay-at-home mum and raise the girls. It was such a humbling experience, but I also quickly understood that I was again distancing myself from my family.

I heard my eldest daughter say, "Dad is always at work, working hard and we don't really get to see him a lot." It broke my heart. It was very hard for me to hear that, and I knew that at some point I needed to make a change or I would run the risk of missing important periods of their growth. I knew I would never be able to get that time back, and this ultimately led me to explore other options to change my career.

I am currently a State Partnership and Stakeholder Manager at The Fathering Project. This is a national charity that transforms children's lives by educating, supporting, and empowering dads. The research shows that children with an effective father or father figure have significantly better social, mental, physical, and academic outcomes. This job allows me the opportunity to have a flexible working arrangement, which allows me to spend precious time with the girls.

When Allayna was nine and Kayla was three, my wife went back to work for the first time in five years and for the first time in Australia since we moved here. I realised that I would now be the parent that would do the morning school runs and the afternoon pick-ups. It was a sobering realisation for me that I would be responsible for most of the school communication and activities, and that this was now part of my daily and weekly tasks. This was going to be a whole different ball game.

I will never forget the first morning we had where I oversaw getting the girls ready for school, which included cereal for breakfast, lunches made, and bags packed. There was also the added pressure of, "Dad I need that form that I brought home two weeks ago for the excursion next week. It needed to be handed in last week, signed by both parents. And I need it today." My daughter only reminded me after my wife left for work. I'm assuming most of us have experienced this at some point?!

I feel privileged in terms of my flexible working arrangements at my current job, allowing me to spend more time with my second daughter. She is in kindy and daycare for four days of the week, and one day of the week she is with me at home. I am truly grateful for the opportunity to be an influence in her life and can ultimately see the difference in our relationship now that Mum has gone back to work.

I love the relationship that I have with my daughters now. No parent is perfect. The stress and the pressure of working in today's world is enormous, and I don't think there is a perfect formula to balance both work and a personal life. As new-age parents, we put ourselves under so much pressure to succeed at parenting, and we often feel that our best is never good enough.

Finding a balance between work and parenting can be a daunting task, but I have found some strategies that have worked for me:

TIME MANAGEMENT

I have become a black belt in time management. Prioritising tasks and creating a schedule or 'hit list' of what I want to achieve during the week allows me dedicated work time, as well as dedicated quality time with my girls.

BOUNDARIES

I have also learned to set boundaries. Establishing clear boundaries between work and family life ensures that work does not encroach upon my personal time. Make sure your colleagues and team are aware of them. This does take a great deal of discipline and flexibility. I also find that communicating openly with my line manager and team about my family commitments is crucial in getting their support when necessary.

SELF-CARE

Finally, remember to take care of yourself first and foremost. Find time for self-care. Allow yourself to catch your breath. The biggest piece of advice my dad gave me later in life was, "Your physical and mental health is the most important thing to support yourself and your family. The organisation you work for will still be standing tomorrow."

To find that balance, you must understand that in any relationship, it is about give and take. In the relationship between work and parenting, find the balance that works for you. I find that when I have work to do and deadlines to meet, I plan my working week better than I did in the past.

My biggest reflection is that I was working so hard to reach a false illusion of 'the higher you climb, the less work you do.' And what I realised was the fact that I was trying to impress people that didn't really know what they wanted out of life. We only have a short period with our kids while they are young, we need to make the most of that time with a focused intention.

DAVID TAYLOR

AS A POLICE OFFICER, I HAVE SEEN SO MANY TIMES THE NEGATIVE EFFECTS AN ABSENT FATHER HAS ON A CHILD, AND THERE ARE NUMEROUS STUDIES TOUTING THE LONG-LASTING EFFECT A PRESENT AND SUPPORTIVE FATHER HAS ON THE DEVELOPMENT OF CHILDREN.

David, a father of two beautiful children who manage to keep him on his toes, considers himself a part-time worker and part-time stay-at-home dad. He has been a police officer for 15 years, choosing a career that enables him to do the things that are important to him, such as travelling with his family or spending time with the kids. David believes time is our most precious resource; it's something you are constantly spending, and it's something you can't get back. He encourages people to be mindful of where they invest it.

DAVID TAYLOR

AUTHOR NAME: DAVID TAYLOR
POSITION: POLICE OFFICER
BUSINESS INDUSTRY: POLICE FORCE / GOVERNMENT
LINKEDIN: LINKEDIN.COM/IN/DAVID-TAYLOR-355806228

My name is David, and I have two children, Olivia (7) and Carter (4). I am currently typing this up on my laptop as I watch Olivia in her weekly gymnastics class while Carter eats dinner next to me. My wife, Susan, is at home sleeping before another night shift in the Perth Children's Hospital Emergency Department, one of four shifts this week, effectively rendering me a solo parent for the week. Such is life when you're married to a shift worker (doctor).

I am the eldest of two boys. My mum grew up in rural Western Australia, and my dad was born in Perth but moved around a bit due to his dad's employment with the Department of Civil Aviation, notably living on the Cocos Keeling Islands for about 18 months. Mum worked for the Commonwealth Bank and stopped working when I was born and was a stay-at-home mum until my brother and I were both in high school, where she returned to the bank on a part-time basis. Dad left school at 15 due to a lack of interest and started working, having various jobs. At one stage, he followed in his father's footsteps and worked for Civil Aviation, which had a project in Papua New Guinea, where Mum and Dad met. After I was born, Dad enrolled in night school and spent many nights completing his high school diploma after I was asleep. Dad continued to be the main source of income for the family, working full-time.

Mum and Dad were actively involved in our education and after-school activities. Mum was engaged with the P&C during primary school; she served as the assistant coach/manager for our tee-ball teams and was always there yelling out encouragement to my brother and me at every sports or swimming carnival. During high school, Dad took on the role with P&C and ended up being the president during my final year of high school. He was consistently present for us on the weekends at our various sporting activities. My brother and I were both in the music program at high school, which included an annual camp away. Every second year usually ended up being an interstate trip, or in the case of my first one, internationally to New Zealand, which involved a lot of fundraising by the school to fund the trip. Dad became the primary organiser for a mouse racing night and sold tickets to many of his friends and colleagues. The funds raised by the night were proportionately distributed to the number of tickets sold by each student. I am fairly sure that more than half the attendees got their tickets from Dad that night.

As much as Dad worked long hours, it never felt like he wasn't there. You could count on both my parents being there on the sidelines at every sports game, carnival, or certificate presentation.

Growing up, Mum and Dad didn't have a lot of money, but we never felt poor. Mum and Dad were always looking for ways to make an extra dollar here and there; these days, you'd call them side hustles. They would do things like working at the elections as Polling Place Managers, lawn mowing, and general maintenance on my uncle's rental properties. The most interesting was when my uncle, who lived in South Hedland (North-Western Australia), picked up a contract for native seed picking as part of a mining rehabilitation project. When the school holidays came around, we set off at 4:00am for the 1,600km (1,000 miles) drive north to my uncle's house. Over the course of the next two weeks, my brother and I helped picking native seeds for this contract – we picked enough seeds to fund the installation of a swimming pool at our house! Worth it!

While Mum wasn't working, holidays for us meant camping, fishing, and exploring Western Australia. As far as I can remember, every Easter school holidays, we would pack up the car and set off at 4:00am to Warroora Station on the Ningaloo Coast, where we would meet up with the rest of the family. Nanna and Grandpa were usually already there with their caravan, and Uncle Ian would drive down from South Hedland with his family. Because it was Easter, Mum would set up an Easter egg hunt for us in the bush, which was great in theory but realistically if it wasn't the heat that got to them before we did, it was Uncle Ian's dog who would sniff out the trail and try to eat the eggs, wrapper and all!

For me, it was never a question of if I would have kids, but when. Whenever I thought about having my own children, I harboured a strong desire to be actively involved and present in their lives. As I write this chapter and reflect on my own childhood, I can now see that this desire stems from my upbringing. Mum and Dad remain significant parts of my life and are embracing their new roles as Nanna and Grandpop!

I am a Police Officer with the Western Australia Police Force and a reservist in the Australian Army. As a police officer, I am fortunate to have six weeks of annual leave each year, some of which I can carry over to the next year. When Susan and I started trying for kids, I accumulated leave before Olivia was born, intending to spend the first eight weeks at home with Susan and Olivia. Adding to the adventure, we decided to renovate the kitchen before Olivia arrived. Like most renovations, the timeline stretched, and the installation for our new cabinets was scheduled about two weeks before Olivia was due. Susan was managing well through the third trimester and continued working until she was 37 weeks pregnant. She even had a baby shower planned for the weekend after she stopped working. On the day of the baby shower, Susan started feeling some uncomfortable Braxton Hicks contractions, which eased when she moved around. After the baby shower, they became stronger, prompting us to go to the hospital. Olivia was born the next day, nearly three weeks early.

As the kitchen renovations were still ongoing, I had to pop home when Olivia was two days old to finish the demolition myself with the help of Dad. Olivia had trouble feeding, and we ended up staying in the hospital for a full week to try and work that out. For Olivia's first few weeks at home, our kitchen consisted of a sandwich press, slow cooker, and a microwave, with dishes being washed in the bathroom.

Being home with Olivia and Susan for the first eight weeks was amazing. Olivia's feeding problems continued; she would happily feed from a bottle but struggled to latch onto Susan. Susan was pumping every time Olivia was hungry, but we didn't want Susan to miss out on feeding and bonding with Olivia. So, we tried to pump when Olivia was asleep, and when she was hungry, Susan could attempt to feed her and then offer her a bottle. Eventually, we discovered that a tongue tie was the reason behind Olivia not being able to latch. I can still remember the emotions I felt and saw in Susan when she was finally able to feed Olivia. This was one of those moments I was glad I was there for.

Because I was home all the time, I developed a very strong bond with Olivia, and she was happy to be settled by either myself or Susan. As with most newborns, Olivia's day and night routines were reversed. Once she was feeding from the breast, Susan would do the night feeds between midnight and 5:00am, leaving me to sleep. When Olivia woke at 5:00am, I would get up, change her nappy, and take her to Susan for a quick feed. Then, I would put her in the baby carrier with some spare milk and take the dog for a walk around our local neighbourhood, leaving Susan to get a few more hours of sleep. I fed Olivia the bottle when she woke up, giving Susan a solid couple of hours of sleep. The dog was living her best life, getting daily hour-plus long walks along the river!

I thoroughly enjoyed the early days of being a new father, and if I could have had more time at home, I would have! I strongly recommend that every new dad spends as much time off work as they can. When Carter was born, I was able to take four weeks off. My favourite memory from that time was when Olivia came to the hospital with her auntie and met Carter for the first time; the look on her face is something that I will always cherish.

We were expecting Carter to have difficulties in breastfeeding as he was born with a cleft lip, but he was able to feed straight from birth and fed like a champ! With the unexpectedly easy process of feeding him and his solid three-hourly routine of eating and sleeping, at three weeks old, we packed up the car and drove to Shark Bay for a two-week camping trip with my parents! It's quite the experience sleeping in a tent with a three-week-old! Almost every photo of Susan has Carter latched on, having a feed.

WA Police has flexible work practices in place, particularly as it relates to part-time arrangements and flexible working hours. This is somewhat difficult to manage due to the dynamic nature of policing and the requirement to see a job through to completion. At the time Olivia was born, I was stationed at the Regional Operations Group. My roster involved a lot of nights and weekends, and it was quite common for me to get involved in a job that required me to stay on for sometimes 10 or 12 extra hours.

When it was time for me to return to work after my eight weeks at home with Susan and Olivia, an opportunity arose for me to take on a higher duties role that was Monday to Friday for a three-month period. Adding this to the nearly two months of leave I took meant that I was home pretty much every night for the first five months after Olivia was born. This gave Susan some extra stability during the tough newborn stage. Shortly after that role finished, I transferred to our district control centre, working fixed hours of two days, two nights, and then four days off. Of all the rosters I have worked, this one felt like I was barely at work, giving me the ability to be present at home and offer Susan a lot of support. The roster also enabled Susan to take on some casual work around my shifts, eventually returning to work on a part-time basis when Olivia was about 18 months old. I think her being able to work while not giving up breastfeeding was good for her overall well-being as well as keeping her current in the workplace for when she eventually returned to work.

Susan went back to work part-time when Carter was 18 months old. She remained part-time until Carter was three and a half. At this stage, Susan and I were both working shift work, including night shifts. There was a point where both our rosters required us to be on night shift at the same time. Between sleeping, working, and school, it meant that Olivia and Carter wouldn't see Susan and me for nearly three days. This was a catalyst for me seeking out a Monday to Friday role, as managing two varying shift patterns is a monumental task, and it is not fair on the kids to not see either of their parents for days.

When Carter was three and a half, Susan and I reversed roles: she moved to full-time work, and I dropped back to part-time. A primary motivator for this change was to allow Susan to progress in her training and career. In my part-time role, I work fixed days with fixed hours. All the kids' before and after-school care and activities are based around my rostered days of work and availability. If Susan happens not to be working during those times, it's a bonus. By setting things up this way, we don't have to juggle based on Susan's shifts, giving the kids some stability and making life, in general, easier for both Susan and me.

When Carter was born, Susan was approaching the stage in her training where she was ready to sit her exams, enabling her to progress in her career. Typically, this involves around 12 months of continuous study leading up to the written component of the exams. When Carter was around six months old, Susan began her studies while I was still working full-time. Thankfully, I had an understanding with my boss who allowed me to take single days of leave every Wednesday, allocating the entire day to Susan to study on top of nightly study sessions. I worked normal office hours and took on as many home duties as I could to allow Susan to focus on her studies. We threw absolutely everything we could at Susan's success in these exams. It is not uncommon for people to sit these exams 2-3 times before passing. Susan got through both the written and clinical components on her first try. We were fortunate that, in addition to my long service leave days, both sets of grandparents would take the kids while I was at work to give Susan additional days for study.

Even before Susan and I had kids, I always wanted to be a big part of my children's lives. On reflection, I would say this is largely due to how involved my parents were in my own childhood. My Spotify playlist features "Cats in the Cradle," the Ugly Kid Joe version, and "Father and Son" by Cat Stevens. Both of these songs hit pretty hard, not only as a father but also as a son. For me, they serve as a reminder of how quickly time goes by and to make the most of the time you have. I usually find myself giving the kids an extra hug or making plans to catch up with my parents when I listen to them.

If there's a moment that makes me thankful for the time I have with my kids, it would have to be every time Olivia or Carter looks up from whatever activity they're doing, and you can see them seeking out my face in the crowd. The way their faces light up when they see me watching them is exactly why I do whatever I can to be there. Being there the day Olivia rode her bike for the first time without training wheels, and seeing Carter cast his own fishing rod are both top 10 moments. Parenthood is an emotional rollercoaster. When I get home from work, both kids drop what they're doing and run full speed to give me a hug. Occasionally, our house is filled with sounds of screaming, but those times are far outweighed by the laughter and screams of joy.

I am currently at the point where I am considering a career

transition, but when I think of our journey up to this point, doing anything differently would mean that many of those memorable moments wouldn't have happened.

Even prior to having children, I have always stuck by the mantra of, "Work to live, not live to work." Anytime I did overtime, it was to fund our next holiday or do renovations on our house. Work is important to me, but it isn't everything, and sadly, most employers will forget who you were within a month or so of you leaving. I read somewhere that 90% of the time you spend with your kids is before they turn 18. That's a staggering statistic and really puts into perspective how much time you are missing out on by being at work. As a police officer, I have seen so many times the negative effects an absent father has on a child, and there are numerous studies touting the long-lasting effect a present and supportive father has on the development of children.

JASON FRISHMAN

IF YOU ARE A DAD WORKING OUTSIDE OF THE HOUSE, IT HAS TO BE ABOUT THE LITTLE INTENTIONAL MOMENTS, THE ROUTINES, RHYTHMS, AND RITUALS THAT YOU CREATE TO DEMONSTRATE SAFETY, LOVE, AND CONNECTION WITH YOUR KIDS.

Jason received a doctorate from William James College (formerly the Massachusetts School of Professional Psychology) where he studied Narrative and Postmodern therapies. He also obtained his Master's degree from Georgia College and State University for Adventure Therapy. He is currently a member of a consensus-based group psychotherapy practice based in Burlington, Vermont and the founder of JourneyMen, a community of fathers dedicated to partnership, connection and growth. Jason believes that our lives are adventurous, and we can and should be active, engaged authors of our own adventure stories!

With a passionate focus on supporting men to challenge our cultural narratives of masculinity and fatherhood, Jason helps men to powerfully connect with themselves, one another and the people they purport to love the most - their partners and children!

JASON FRISHMAN

NAME: JASON FRISHMAN
ROLE: FOUNDER AND LEAD COACH
COMPANY: JOURNEYMENCONNECTEDFATHERS
LINKEDIN: WWW.LINKEDIN.COM/IN/DRJASONSFRISHMAN/

SARAH:
Can you start by telling me about what you do and how you got into it?

JASON:
Absolutely. First off, I'm a papa to two sons, Micah and Isaiah, who are 15 and 12 right now. I'm a partner to my wife, Shana, and we live in a rural area of Northeastern United States in Vermont. Very intentionally, this was a place that I chose to live when I was a kid and have wanted to be here forever. I'm a psychologist of 25 years, which is something that I knew I wanted to do even as a child. I love it. That being said, I have always been a little bit of a different psychologist than most. My master's degree is in Adventure Therapy, so it's a style of therapy using activities, experiences, and metaphors.

SARAH:
Amazing.

JASON:
It's pretty amazing, yeah. It's a really powerful use of metaphor

and activity using both your body and your mind in different ways. It was amazing for me to find that program – currently, it's an international field. I did my master's and then, after hiking for almost six months on the Appalachian Trail (a 2000+ mile trail along the eastern coast of the United States) and working as a therapist for several years, I went back to earn my doctorate and focused on a unique perspective called Narrative Therapy, which you may have heard of … A lot of great work in narrative therapy came from Australia and New Zealand.

Narrative therapy is founded on the idea that our character, who we are in relation to ourselves and others, is based on the stories that we tell about ourselves and that are told about us from an individual level all the way to a cultural level. We have an impact on the stories that represent us and our relationships and we can have agency to author our own stories and the way that we live. What if there is a story in our lives that doesn't describe us in the way we see ourselves or want to be seen? What if that story becomes so 'popular' that it overshadows any other description of us? How can we stand up to stories that are overshadowing our preferred ways of being in this world? So, there's a politicized element to narrative therapy, right? Because if there are dominant stories that are suppressing or oppressing other stories in who we are, we have to stand up to them. Narrative therapy encourages us all to stand up to dominant, oppressive stories in our lives. It's activism on all levels.

SARAH:
Yeah. I totally get the concept.

JASON:
So, for almost 25 years, my focus in therapy was boys, men, and families. And I mainly worked in residential treatment centers and outpatient centers in hospitals, schools, and clinics. And, until I had my own kids, I was working mostly with kids and

families. At that point, I chose to see less kids. I wanted to give my 'child energy' to our kids and our friends' children. And so I started seeing more older men and then started working almost exclusively with fathers. About five years ago while working for a not-for-profit group therapy practice in Burlington, Vermont, I started my own business coaching men and offering coaching for fathers. I focus on helping dads become more connected at home with themselves, their kids, and their partners. As a father, if the foundation at home is strong, you can do better out in the world. You can do more good for men, for their communities, and for everyone. It has been really powerful. The whole concept of my coaching program is that we're writing new narratives for men and masculinity and fatherhood. And we're writing new stories because the stories that we have now—the 'Hero's Journey,' the 'kings,' the 'warriors'—all of these stories, they're actually quite damaging to men and boys. As we all know, damaged boys and men become damaging boys and men. The patriarchy does not like men either.

It's working powerfully with guys who are open to this idea, helping them understand that their true adventure is at home with family, the people they purport to love the most. I host a virtual inn where guys can come in from their adventure at home and drop their shoulders and share real stories and real strategies for connecting more powerfully. I'm still working as a psychotherapist. I'm doing that while I'm working and building this coaching program for fathers. And over the past years I've had other entrepreneurial adventures, typically around food. I'm a cook and I love feeding people. I've started a bunch of food businesses over the years.

With my coaching program, I keep telling the guys that I want to do a retreat with them. We're planning one for the spring, and I have said, very selfishly, that I want to do the retreat so that I can cook the guys all a meal. I just want to cook them dinner!

SARAH:

What an added bonus for them all, ha-ha! I'd be very happy with that. Tell me about your childhood and how you were raised.

JASON:
I grew up outside of New York City with my mom and my dad and a younger sister, and we were in the suburbs, and I come from a New York Jewish family. I don't know if this will be resonant for you or for any readers, but a New York Jewish family is a culture in and of itself. Summer camp is also an important piece of my childhood.

SARAH:
I worked at a summer camp in Northern Michigan and absolutely loved it!

JASON:
Amazing! Yeah, so, I went to camp. My parents actually met in summer camp, so it was important to them that we went. We didn't have a lot of money at the time, so my mom actually worked there just so we could go. It was that important to her and to my dad.

My childhood was really quite wonderful. At home, my parents were very intentional and very loving. My dad is a social worker, my mom is a teacher. They're both good with kids. But I found out only recently that when they were thinking about having me—I'm the oldest—they got together with a bunch of their friends who were also going to have kids, and they hired a parenting expert to come to their house and run a parenting group so that all these young kids—and I mean, they *were* very young—could be ready and could understand what to do. So, they really were very intentional.

SARAH:
Love that!

JASON:

They're very intentional on so many levels that I remember from childhood and we had lots of traditions. I have strong memories of everything from our Jewish traditions to just little, yet meaningful, family things. I lived in a town where there weren't a lot of Jewish folk, so there was antisemitism – there were things that I remember not feeling great about at school.

I wasn't particularly popular, but I found my place. I think it goes back to a lot—I'd never thought about it this way—but it goes back to what I was telling you about my coaching program, which is, if your foundation is strong, you can do more elsewhere. At school, I was not particularly happy, but because my foundation at home was strong—I don't want to say confident because I wasn't confident—but I was solid. I was solid enough.

SARAH:
Yeah, it gives you an internal confidence, that internal security.

JASON:
Exactly. And because of that, I went outside of my school, I found a youth group. I found friends from camp and many of them are people I'm still friends with today. I have strong and very positive feelings about my childhood and particularly my parents. I have warm memories about growing up in New York.

SARAH:
Lovely. That's really nice! And when your boys arrived, how did you and your partner balance that, and how did you decide what your roles were going to be as parents?

JASON:
It's interesting you say that because we were intentional. And it's interesting because the decision that we made actually looks like traditional gender roles, even though that's not what we believe in, it's just what has worked for our family. We made a decision that

I was going to be the working parent and actually—wait, this is really important because language to us is very, very important—we never actually said the words 'working parent', I don't know why I said that just then, but I was the parent who was going to the office and she was the parent who was working at home.

That's actually quite important. We would correct people when our kids were babies. We never said, "Papa's going to work," because what does that say about her staying home? We always said, "Papa's going to the office." We did that even when the kids were infants, and we corrected friends. We made it an activist thing. We were standing up to the story that the stay-at-home parent isn't 'working.' If you think about it, the only reason I am able to go off to the office is that my wife works at home. She's taken care of the things that need to be done for living. Usually, people think about it the other way around—we can only eat because I bring in money. Well, no, it's much more than that.

SARAH:
And it's actually my experience, it's a harder job being at home with your children doing everything at home than going out to the office.

JASON:
Oh yes... I was fortunate that during the month that my oldest son was born, I took my licensure exam and passed it. I left my internship at the local hospital and I joined a group practice.

And fortunately, we have a loving community here. That was really helpful. But that was something that was very intentional. I was able to take some time off because I had left one job and I was starting a new practice, so I was home for a little while with my wife. I think the thing that was really hard is that I had felt a big pressure to get my practice going so that we could have some earnings. I would go into the office even though I didn't have a lot of clients. And it was challenging for my wife and I at the time, she was feeling it more. She was at home doing the harder job, and I was here in the office not seeing anyone. It was a real challenge for us. And to this day, it's sort of something we sometimes still struggle thinking about. But that being said, I agree that she does—and did—the harder job for sure. We strive to remain intentional when it comes to the 'work' of family life. As I said, I have these strong memories of my own childhood with these important rituals and important moments—'bookmark moments' is what I call them. And we spend a lot of time creating that with our kids.

SARAH:
And it's really important to have that. In terms of your working hours, I know with regards to having clinics and stuff, you can be a little bit more flexible, so did you make sure you were kind of home at a decent time for dinner and things like that? So, that you have that presence as well?

JASON:
Yeah, as a family, we do eat dinner a little later than most of our friends, that's for sure. Especially because I'm a cook and one of my first specialties as a therapist was family meals. I helped clients work on family meals and how important that is. I would say even now that 95% of our meals arc caten together as a family.

I always came home for that, and for bedtime. I've been able to set my schedule where my wife and I split who gets the kids to school and things like that. And I have always—we did this very early on and we've been doing this forever—kept Monday night as 'boys night.' Monday nights I make a quick dinner for all of us, including my wife, and she either goes out with friends or takes time to herself or whatever she wants. My boys and I either go fishing, or we play a game, or we watch a Star Wars movie or something. Our night is Monday night. And so that's something that starts off every week. We always do it.

SARAH:

Yeah, that's lovely. And you getting that quality time with them while she gets a break is a good balance, right?

JASON:

Absolutely. And I would say the other part is that I have another night in the week where I sort of get a break. We are very intentional with the way that we look at and try to respect our time. That's not to say that there aren't problems – there certainly are, and we can argue over the mental load and how to take care of things and all of that. But there's the conversation, there is the time that we take to make it work.

And the compromise between the two, which is huge, I think. Creating that gender balance in a workplace needs to start from home. If you don't have it at home, how's it ever going to be able to translate into a workplace? And that's where I think it's so important to create that balance at home where you've got that shared responsibility because otherwise a female goes out to work and then she's got to come home and still look after an entire household and do everything else. It's impossible.

SARAH:

Absolutely.

JASON:

I'll say that I probably need to do more at home, but I'm working on it.

SARAH:

No one's perfect.

JASON:

That's true. But it's important to say that a lot of what we do, even in the home, a lot of what men do are things that are more visible, and a lot of what women do doesn't get seen or noticed as much. And I'm working on doing this even more and being better about it, but acknowledging things and noticing things and doing it in front of my sons because it's important that they see that. Right? I used to joke that I would make this gourmet meal, and until I met my wife, I would put it on paper plates. It is very important to her to make things beautiful. And the truth is, if I were to put it on paper plates, people would notice that they're on paper plates. But when we put it on nice plates in a nice room, they don't notice that as much. They still talk about the food. The idea is that we want to make sure that the ambiance, and the experience, and that my wife really puts a lot of love and attention into our home is just as acknowledged as the meal, especially by my sons.

SARAH:
Yeah, absolutely. And in terms of how you want them to be raised, you've just said it really – you've been quite intentional in terms of not creating those stereotypical gender roles as such, so that they'll grow up and see how that balance can be and what they can be doing themselves.

JASON:
And in some ways, it's still a challenge because in many ways our lives do look like typical gender roles. My wife is doing more of the home stuff. I'm doing more of the stuff in the office. We're having conversations with our kids and we're talking about it intentionally. I talk with a lot of dads and often say, "Look, it's not about the actual chores. It's not about the actual work you're doing. It's about how do you acknowledge what gets done and what needs to get done?" How do you acknowledge, how do you see, how do you choose, and how it's our responsibility to notice things that we would never notice otherwise? Because we, as men, haven't been socialized to notice.

SARAH:

Yeah, yeah. Absolutely. And if you were to offer a key bit of advice to dads out there, what would it be?

JASON:

I think for dads that go to an office or work outside of the home, I think the best advice that I've ever given, and that I got from my parents my whole life, is remember that life is a long game. We're not looking for big, epic, momentary things. That massive week-long vacation is not going to create the foundation of relationships that you truly want. Consistency and long-term planning is the real foundation for sustainable, meaningful conversations and relationships. I have a document that I give out to people, it's a list of the fastest ways to connect with your kids; there are 10 of them on there. If you do every one, it takes less than 15 minutes. If you are a dad working outside of the house, it has to be about the little intentional moments, the routines, rhythms, and rituals that you create to demonstrate safety, love, and connection with your kids.

And the quality time doesn't have to be quantity. I have said the same 12 words to both of my kids every single night of their life before bedtime: "I love you for always and forever, you are my sweet one." Even when we're not in the same place, they get a phone call or a nightly note. It's the practice of loving and loving consistently – even when we may be arguing or unhappy with one another. The commitment is a long-term process for a long-term relationship. My 15-year-old and I, there are times when we argue, there are times when we go at it pretty strongly, but even if we're angry with one another, even if it's at bedtime, I'll go over to them and share, "I'm going to say it, okay. I'll say it to you." And I say those 12 words. And it's an amazing and powerful lesson that no matter how big of an argument we're having, no matter how much of a jerk I was or whatever, I plan on knowing him and loving him for the rest of our lives.

SARAH:
Absolutely.

JASON:
And I will always say this, and I will always mean it. I think, to me, it's the idea that it's long-term. I still write notes in both their lunches every single day. And if you have these little special things that are daily, weekly, monthly, yearly, those are the things that I remember from my childhood. You don't need big, you need committed consistency.

SARAH:
Absolutely. Yeah. Amazing. Oh, I love it. Is there anything else that you want to add?

JASON:
I remember growing up—sorry, I have one more story—one of my favorite times growing up is when we did a movie night and made popcorn. We went downstairs and all four of us watched a movie and my dad would lay down on the couch. The space behind his legs and the back of the couch was called the back porch, and my sister or I would get to cuddle with him sitting there and watch the movie. It still brings back a feeling of coziness and safety... And my kids grew up doing the same thing with me. I remember we didn't even go out to the movies much, but these ideas, it was meaningful and memorable for me to sit with my family, watch a movie, and eat popcorn. It was as memorable as if we were doing something major and it felt like a big thing because we were together, they were with us. It's so cool because the traditions or rituals or things like that are basically anything you choose to do intentionally, that gains meaning over time. And it doesn't have to be epic or legendary or any of those things. One time I forgot a note in my 15-year old's lunch and he was like, "Where's my note?"

I responded with a joke, "Yeah, you don't even read it." Without hesitation, he said, "Yeah, but it's nice to see it." I've done all sorts of really fun things with their notes too, so I get a kick out of it. It's important to note here that these little, intentional giving moments feel good for my boys and they feel good to me as well. It goes both ways.

SARAH:
Absolutely, it makes you feel good and it makes him feel good. Well Jason, it's been such a pleasure. Thank you for your time and I will look forward to doing more work together in the future.

BRAD RAYNOR

> VULNERABILITY IS A SUPERPOWER FOR ME, AND I FEEL FOR US ALL. BEING VULNERABLE TO MY OWN THOUGHTS, ACTIONS, AND WILLINGNESS TO SEE THERE ARE OTHER WAYS OF DOING THINGS HELPED US RAISE TWO AMAZING ADULTS.

Brad, the father of twins, Holly and Owen, and husband to Kate, is the founder of two thriving consultancies, Cognito and BNR Leadership. His specialty lies in expertly teaching and coaching leaders to develop mastery-level skills that unlock dynamic engagement and collaborative commitment. These skills empower leaders to cultivate high-performing, independent, and healthy teams, transforming complex organisations and unlocking their own freedom. For 30 years, Brad has been an expert teacher, mentor, and coach, specialising in behavioural engagement, human leadership, and organisational design optimisation. He has delivered outstanding results in some of the most complex workplace environments in Australia, Asia, and Africa. Brad has successfully led multi-million-dollar organisations through transitions, being taught and mentored by giants in the education and leadership world such as Prof. Barry Bennett, Prof. Michal Fullan, and Peter Smillanich, gaining advanced leadership experience and understandings that now underpin his executive teaching, coaching, and mentoring workshop programs.

BRAD RAYNOR

AUTHOR NAME: BRADLEY RAYNOR
BUSINESS NAME: COGNITO
POSITION: DIRECTOR
BUSINESS INDUSTRY: BUSINESS CONSULTANCY
WEBSITE: WWW.COGNITHQ.COM.AU
LINKEDIN: LINKEDIN.COM/IN/BRADLEY-RAYNOR-16341A182

Being a biological father can sometimes just happen. It's a job that can be given to just about any man. But being a *good* dad is a choice that needs to be made, every day.

Through this short story, I wanted to talk about choice, about choosing to try to be a 'good dad,' and how we wanted to inspire our beloved twins to choose a life they want and not just follow what we think is right. Giving my twins 'choice' is one of my deepest desires in life. I wanted to share my journey, share my failures, share my successes, and share how I had to become vulnerable to show up as a good dad.

Vulnerability, in my opinion, is your greatest superpower—a powerful and painful superpower that can help us be good dads and good parents. Being vulnerable is about the best advice I can give to any dad out there. Oh, and buy all the power tools for the jobs you will need to do around the house, ideally before they are born, because once they come, your priorities will alter so much that the drill you need to hang the clay hand imprints on the wall will not be bought until they are old enough to use it themselves!

I use the term 'good dad' over 'great dad' because I have come to realise that being good enough is the best that we can do. If each day we aim to be good, and tomorrow a bit better, and better again the day after that, then that's the best we can do to be the best we can be. Our metaphorical candle can only burn so bright, and that is good enough.

I am a (good) dad to boy/girl twins, Owen and Holly. I'm super proud of them in every way. During the ultrasounds, they were called T1 and T2, and the excitement that came with their birth was like nothing I, or my wife Kate, had ever experienced before, nor in the 24 years since. We didn't want to know their gender because it didn't matter. We chose two sets of names, knowing that when they were born, we would know which name to give each one when we held them for the first time. All we wanted was to take our babies home and be a family.

Choosing to be a good dad was a conscious mission I took on from the moment Kate shared that she was pregnant. It was easy to work out my purpose in the beginning; "I want to be the best dad and give my kids everything!" I embraced it like it was my life mission. First, I decided, I will learn everything I can about what being a dad involves. I will learn how to physically care for them and prepare financially and psychologically for their arrival. Kate and I read books, did courses together, and made plans.

Having the twins was the best thing to happen to us, despite how hard it was (if you're a parent of twins, you understand). We were both just grateful it wasn't triplets! As we started our parenting journey, we made plans together to help us through the tough times. Those plans were great fallbacks and saved us so many times, especially when we were so tired, we literally could not think.

Following routine and adjusting it based on the needs of the day became our mantra. Choosing to prepare and then choosing to work together, listening to each other, and being vulnerable to the truth was invaluable. This changed my purpose as a dad for the better. I went from, "I want to be the best dad and give my kids everything," to "I want to be a good husband first, and a good dad second." In that order. It was—and is—important to care for your wife equally, if not more important, than looking after the babies. That was one of the most important lessons I learned.

Twins can take turns crying, take turns sleeping, feeding— everything! Whatever you do, it's double, and not necessarily at the same time. It's a simple truth that every parent of twins or multiples can relate to. When one stops, there is a moment where you relax, find peace, knowing your beloved baby is at rest, almost nod off to sleep yourself, and then the other one starts. There were times when the twins, whom I love more than life itself, were crying, and we needed to let them cry themselves to sleep. Kate and I knew that if we just let them cry after their midnight feed (that took over an hour of tag team effort), for just 10 minutes, they would sleep for five hours. And once they were asleep, they would grow, rest, develop, and thrive. We needed to be cruel to be kind. I was also acutely aware that a lot of the time, I had to get up in four hours to travel 50kms to teach complex students, then drive home, help with the house, and know there was an 8:00pm and then a midnight feed to assist with.

There were times that I remember wanting to sleep and feeling concerned that the lack of sleep would stop me from being awesome for my students. I remember being so consumed by their crying and worrying so much about them. I knew they were dry, clean, fed, healthy, and safe, but I was so confused that they just would not stop. Why were they doing this to us? I transitioned through emotions from choosing to be the best dad and a loving husband to being frustrated and overwhelmed. I would yell out to my six-month-old twins, "Just tell me what you want!"

The pressure we put on ourselves to be the best dad, the best provider for the family, the best at our job, and the best loving and devoted husband... it's a lot! And sometimes it's more than we can handle. It's not easy to admit that yelling through the pillow at my beloved twins (in another room) out of sheer frustration happened multiple times before they turned one. I had to really look at myself, examine what I was doing and why. I had to recognise what was happening and face the reality that it was not them who had the problem—it was me. It was then that I truly learned that I wouldn't be 'the-best-dad-ever-who-never-got-upset.' I just had to be a good dad who knew how to manage and regulate his emotions.

Kate knew all too well what I was going through. She understood my frustrations and reminded me that the twins were just babies, and I was projecting my adult emotions onto them. I knew this (after all, I was a teacher who specialised in complex behavioural issues in other children), but I had let those feelings swallow me up. I was embarrassed and ashamed, even though at the time I tried to justify myself. In that moment, and all those that followed, I had to choose to be vulnerable and change the way I reacted to difficult situations at home. I had to look deep within myself and choose to regulate myself—something that was not easy at 2:00am in the morning, I can tell you! I realised that vulnerability was a superpower.

The twins progressed through primary and then secondary school. I wanted them to be empowered to choose any future they wanted, in whatever context that looked like. Holly and Owen share a deep bond, having been in the same class throughout their primary years as we moved about the state. Despite being twins with a strong connection, they are also two very individual people who love each other deeply and wish to explore the world in their unique ways. Our passion has always been to allow them to thrive independently, collaborate effectively, celebrate one another, and be each other's strongest cheerleader. I aimed for them to excel in school, ensuring they have the ability to shape their future with a good education, learning *how* to think, not just *what* to think, and understanding who they are.

I was a passionate classroom teacher, and when they were

young, I transitioned into a role as a teacher trainer, guiding other educators to accelerate student progression. I had the privilege of being selected for a specialised program, where I underwent six years of training by internationally recognised experts in engagement, commitment, leadership, coaching, adult and child education, leadership skills, and organisational renewal. Armed with this expertise, I became a specialist, sharing proven methods to accelerate student development and engage staff in fostering social, emotional, and academic growth in all students. Schools sought me out due to my success and what I could help them achieve. However, despite all my knowledge and efforts, I couldn't get my own children to apply the methods I taught others. I shared, modelled, assisted their friends and family, cajoled, bribed, encouraged, made deals, threatened, and even felt frustration and discouragement. Then, with the wisdom of my wife, I realised that I was already getting what I wished for—my twins were choosing to navigate life in their own way. They were deciding how to engage with the world, and in their unique approach, they were thriving. I had to embrace the vulnerability that my way was not the only way.

What they needed was for me to choose to walk beside them and assist them in the ways they needed. They needed me to use questions to unlock their thinking. They needed me to reserve judgment, making it safer for them to figure out what they wanted to do and how they wanted to do it. The more I did this, the more they thrived. They needed me to be vulnerable, holding onto my beliefs, my thinking, and what I wanted to help them embrace their own choices.

The twins thrived in school. They learned how to manage complex situations, navigate difficult people, make good friends, and understand what was important to them. It was not my way; it was their way. It was a good way, and they chose it. We cannot force our views and ways of doing things onto others. The complexity of each individual makes the world more interesting, but it can be a hard pill to swallow when it's your own children, and you just want what's best for them.

Like me, the twins' learning abilities came with a caveat, whereby they took the 'spelling-is-optional' approach combined with questionable grammatical skills (thankfully, this story has been edited by professionals!). I wanted them to have a much easier path than I did and to not feel the same shame and struggles I had when it came to writing and communication. Subconsciously, I imposed my expectations and hopes on them rather than supporting them to be the best they can be. I learned that their shame came when I didn't accept their honest efforts as good enough. I had to be vulnerable, look inside myself, and not project my desires (or hurt and shame) onto them. When I chose to respect their efforts, they felt accepted. Being vulnerable gave them the freedom to do school their way, which over the years gave them the ability to choose when, how, and what to engage in. They got the freedom we wanted for them.

During both their university studies, Owen had an opportunity to walk the Bibbulmun Track end-to-end with his aunt, who was turning 50. Due to the timing, this would require him to defer his Environmental Science degree for a year. He brought the idea to us to discuss and was surprised, even a little shocked, when we enthusiastically encouraged him to defer, take the year, go on an adventure. He soon realised it was the power to choose and take hold of his life that we were passionate about, not his studies. Vulnerability has allowed me to get out of his way and allowed him to walk back to us again.

The twins, now adults, have been able to choose who they love, what work they do, what studies they want to undertake, and how they live their lives. While education and work are not universal measures of success for all, the fact that the twins have chosen to complete university degrees and are in graduate programs, choosing to work in areas they are passionate about, is a joy-filled delight to us. They are choosing their path, and this is everything we wanted for them. This is because my wife and I chose to be vulnerable. Well, the truth is she was always very good at vulnerability and helped me develop it over the years as a father. I embrace looking inside myself, demolish any projections, and let go of steering the ship when it wasn't going in the direction I hoped for. Together we chose to support the twins when they were young, when they were working out how to make the right choices for themselves, and we did this by walking by their side and holding their hands—not yelling into pillows or telling them how they should live their lives or forcing world-recognised best learning practices on them, regardless of how much we believe in it.

Vulnerability is a superpower for me, and I feel for us all. Being vulnerable to my own thoughts, actions, and willingness to see there are other ways of doing things helped us raise two amazing adults. Choosing to be vulnerable never stopped me from giving advice and teaching, or sharing what I thought was wisdom, but it did stop me from imposing my expectations. Being vulnerable allowed me to let them fail or fall (no matter how much it hurt to watch) and help them back up when they needed it, regardless of the situation. The most important part of being vulnerable stopped me from choosing their future, which opened up a life of opportunity for them to explore, knowing they will always have their family walking beside them and cheering them on.

CHARLIE MAUGHAN

> TL;DR — you're doing great, stick with it. Because if you're reading this book, it means you care. And that's 95% of parenting.

Charlie is a father to two girls, Frankie and Rae. Currently serving as an Account Director at the marketing communications firm imageseven in Perth, WA, he is additionally an advocate for men's mental health. In this capacity, Charlie holds the position of Vice-President at Mens Talk, a charity dedicated to fostering conversations around wellness and masculinity for all individuals who identify as male.

CHARLIE MAUGHAN

AUTHOR NAME: CHARLIE MAUGHAN
BUSINESS NAME: IMAGESEVEN
POSITION: ACCOUNT DIRECTOR, PEOPLE AND CULTURE
BUSINESS INDUSTRY: MARKETING AND COMMUNICATIONS
WEBSITE: WWW.IMAGESEVEN.COM.AU
LINKEDIN USERNAME: LINKEDIN.COM/IN/CHARLIEMAUGHAN

I am writing this chapter over several Wednesday nights after 9.30pm. This, fittingly, sets the scene for a familiar theme faced by all working dads and mums: time, or the lack thereof. With kids, life becomes very full. From the morning alarm until your head hits the pillow, it's a sprint – to get up, to the gym, and to work so that you are back in time for the school pick-up or the evening routine of dinner, bath, story time, and bed. Then it's time for *you* to eat and put your feet up for a bit before calling it a night, fresh and ready to do it all again tomorrow.

I always wanted to be a dad. I am fortunate to have had a loving and caring father myself, for which I am eternally grateful, knowing that not everyone is quite so lucky. The idea that I could play some small part in nurturing, guiding, and mentoring someone has always appealed to me. Knowing that deep down I, one day, wanted to be a dad—and that I *chose* to be one—has always been a guiding light whenever the going got tough.

No one has the secret sauce for parenting, and every journey is different. When I think of myself pre-kids, a prospective dad with a great deal of love, energy, and time to give, I wonder what kind of advice I would have given him knowing what I know now. Below are my tips to that version of Charlie, and to all budding working parents out there.

TL;DR – you're doing great, stick with it. Because if you're reading this book, it means you care. And that's 95% of parenting.

1. MANY HANDS MAKE LIGHT(ER) WORK

"Teamwork makes the dream work." – John C Maxwell

My wife, Nicki, and I are both sports lovers. We watch, play, and compete. So, it only felt natural that our approach to parenthood would mirror how we faced challenges as a couple—teamwork. Strong teams, in sport, business, and government, are elite communicators. The same applies to relationships. If communication falters and you don't feel you can talk openly and honestly with your partner, cracks will appear.

Nick and I have a code. If one of us says "I'm sad," the TV is switched off, we drop what we're doing and give each other 100% focus. I'm not sure how it started, but it means that we can cut through any preamble and get right into an open and raw conversation. This has been very powerful for us because it also serves as a fuse switch that catches anything before it can compound and become a bigger issue. As working parents, you juggle plenty of responsibilities in your life. If you don't feel like you have that mutual safety net with your partner, then any fall from the proverbial 'high wire' will be exacerbated.

Nick is an extremely honed professional in her own right. She's the breadwinner; an accomplished lawyer at a top firm. That also means she has her own priorities and commitments. Because we see ourselves as a team, we both cover for one another when required.

Becoming working parents meant that we had to change our definition of teamwork. Before, it meant that we did everything together. Now it means that sometimes we are ships in the night.

In reality, we are lifting an equal load and coming together when we can. And should it get too much, we still have our code.

2. FIND YOUR 'ME-TIME' – AND MAKE IT HEALTHY

"You can't pour from an empty cup." – Unknown

Sometimes it all gets too much. Being able to play 'tag' with your partner or someone in your close support network is a good strategy to catch your breath. It isn't selfish. You need to fill up that bucket of love so that you have something to give. Identifying your me-time is crucial to avoid any feelings of building resentment. Being a great parent, successful at work, and a loving partner all at once can be a drain on anyone. Your me-time is the pressure valve that keeps this at bay.

As a side note, becoming a parent made me truly appreciate how difficult it would be to be a single parent. These people are built different, and they deserve every superlative.

A warning: me-time comes with a caveat. When you take it, be prepared to come back at 100%. A working parent's time is stretched enough as it is. Know how long your me-time window is and make sure you get maximum usage—and benefit—from it. Getting organised helps (more on this later).

I said 'make it healthy' because having a healthy mind and body means you can be an even better parent. Parenting isn't a sprint, it's an ultramarathon. You're in it for the long haul and if you can ensure your body is in good working condition, you'll be able to parent for even longer. If that's not enough of an incentive, then the natural endorphin rush that comes post-exercise with Dopamine and Serotonin flooding your system are the perfect stabilisers for when times are tough in other areas of your life.

'Making it healthy' is not to say that you can't have other interests. Sure, it helps if your hobby is somewhat physically active, but if you love the arts or some other creative pursuit then that's great too! Catching up with mates, playing music, or reading a book, it really doesn't matter—just come back at 100%.

As a side note, if you're not a morning person, try to learn how to become one. If I can have my exercise or 'me-time' already done before anyone else in the house is awake, then I know that I've already had it, and can be 100% present for the rest of the day.

3. GRAB A COFFEE AND MAKE A PLAN

"If a man knows not which port he sails, no wind is favourable." – Seneca

Nick and I have a thing called a 'coffee and plan'. It's where we have a long brunch, lots of coffees, no time pressure or distractions, and an honest conversation about what we want from our lives. From there, we chart them out strategically. We have a note saved on Nick's phone from about ten years ago which we laugh at now, because everything we planned, has happened, in the order and timeframe we predicted!

I am not suggesting every inch of your life be planned out, leaving no room for improvisation, freedom, or creativity; but being a working parent means that life becomes a bit of a blur. Suddenly you'll pop your head up and a year has passed. Set those big life goals out with your partner, along with rough timelines. You can then assess your current career and personal trajectories and see if you need to adjust. Then, get to work!

There's a swimming technique called 'sighting'. In open water swimming, you must be able to regularly pop your head up—without breaking stroke—to check that you're heading towards a landmark, buoy, or your ultimate destination. Practice sighting in your personal life. And yes, these 'coffee and plans' become even more precious (and important) when you have kids.

4. BE HONEST WITH YOURSELF AND IDENTIFY YOUR PRIORITIES

"I used to be a juggler, but I lost the balls to do it." – Unknown

I'm not sure where I came across them, but there are two analogies regarding managing competing priorities that have stuck with me and guided my decision making as an adult, partner, and dad.

THE FOUR BURNERS THEORY
BRYAN DYSON'S FIVE BALLS OF LIFE THEORY

David Sedaris's Four Burners Theory is the idea that your life is represented by a stove with four burners. Each burner symbolises a major area of your life:

- Family
- Friends
- Health
- Work

It states that to be successful, you need to cut off one burner, to be *really* successful, you need to cut off two. This metaphor has stuck with me. When something comes up, I can say to myself, "Ok, I'm just going to turn down this burner so that I can focus on another one." When you become a parent, the 'Family' burner is going to need a lot of your attention. Being able to consciously 'turn down' the gas on one of the other burners is a valuable skill. Throughout your life you will go through different stages where some burners need to burn more brightly than others. I'm sure you can agree that burning all burners at 100% is incredibly draining and only really viable short term, or else you burnout. Pun intended.

Bryan Dyson's Five Balls of Life theory is similar, but that there are five balls in life:

- Family
- Friends
- Health
- Spirit (or character)
- Work

Bryan Dyson, former CEO of Coca-Cola, said in a speech to Georgia Institute of Technology that in life, everyone is juggling five balls. All are made of glass except 'Work', which is made of rubber. If you drop the Work ball, it will bounce back. If the other four fall, they'll be scuffed, damaged, or shattered.

I once read somewhere that 'children spell love, T-I-M-E.' The times I remember most fondly with my dad were not when he was coming home just as I was going to bed, but when he took me to the school bus, or came to watch my sports games. My dad worked for a large insurance broker in the centre of London, and only as I've gotten older, have I been able to appreciate the stress he was under. Yet, I will always remember looking to the sideline and seeing him there. He knew that 'Work' would bounce back.

Being a working parent is about organising, prioritising, and compromising. By making conscious decisions about your priorities—week-to-week, month-to-month, year-to-year—you will undo any of undue mental stress you might have about whether you are making the right decisions.

5. TIME TO GET ORGANISED

"The plan is nothing; planning is everything." – *Ocean's Eleven* (2001)

Whenever we enter a period of change—a busy period at work, a new sport season, or a new family/child commitment—Nick and I get to work on building a new schedule. For us, this is a weekly planner that establishes the new status quo in the house, principally:

Our respective 'me-time'

Who's on pick-ups and drop-offs

This planner establishes the baseline (or 'regular') schedule for that period. Here is an example of a recent planner in our household:

Monday	Tuesday	Wednesday	Thursday	Friday	Saturday	Sunday
Nick training Charlie drop-off	Nick training Charlie drop-off	Charlie training Nick drop-off	Charlie training Nick drop-off	Nick training	Charlie training Nick training	Charlie training
Charlie pick-up Nick singing	Nick pick-up Charlie training	Charlie pick-up Nick netball	Charlie pick-up Nick netball			

Of course, you can substitute training for whatever your 'me-time' activity is. If your activity can be done before anyone is awake, even better.

When it comes to organisation, technology is your friend. Use multiple shared Apple/Google calendars with your partner to maintain a living source of truth. We've got eight (!) calendars that sync across our phones to ensure every single commitment is captured—nothing falls off. On Sunday evening, we review the week coming and confirm if the 'regular' schedule is still sufficient, or whether adjustments are needed.

6. GET OFF INSTAGRAM AND OUT OF YOUR HEAD

"Comparison is the thief of joy." – Theodore Roosevelt

The adage rings true—don't compare your everyday to someone else's highlight reel. At 3:00am, blurry-eyed and trying to get a baby to sleep, knowing you have an alarm set for 6:00am, the last thing you need is a display of glossy photos featuring happy, seemingly perfect mums and dads who are more tanned and fit than you, with their smiling children in nauseatingly picturesque getaway locations. The reality? The photo was probably taken just before or after a tantrum, outfit swap, or a messy nappy change.

In addition to the devastating effect it has on women, postnatal depression also effects up to 1 in 10 dads.[1] Blokes, typically, are garbage at talking openly and honestly about emotions. This is steadily changing; however, I urge you to think about, and be able to identify, your support network of mates and family who can lift you up if you're struggling.

As with all things, social media is fine in moderation. If you're feeling the self-doubt creeping in, take a break and instead reach out to your *true* support network—friends and family.

7. IF YOU WANT TO TAKE TIME OFF, DO IT ON YOUR TERMS

"Fatherhood is about the journey, not the destination." – Michael Stadther

I was so excited to become a dad. Our first daughter was born just as the pandemic started which added stress, but even that

---

1 Beyondblue.org.au

couldn't dampen my verve. Little did I know what I was in for. When you have a child, nobody sits you down and says, "Hey, yes, it's going to be amazing. But it's also going to be really bloody hard. And that's normal. You're not alone."

I also wish I knew that newborns *literally cannot see you*. And they can't for weeks. I felt lost in those first few weeks and months as I tried to build this magical connection with this newborn, who clearly wasn't ready. The Hollywood trope that your baby looks into your eyes, and you into theirs, and in that moment your mutual unconditional love is cemented forevermore—yeah, that doesn't happen.

Working for a small/medium firm, I didn't have the additional parental benefits enjoyed by larger companies. I had initially planned to take extended time off – I had even planned to go part-time and work reduced days so I could spend more time with my new family – but I was torn. Opting not to go part time would be an admission of failure that I didn't want to be at home. But on the other hand, if I did go part-time, I was worried that I wouldn't maximise the time.

After lengthy discussions with Nick, we opted against the idea of me going part-time. Nick had some great parental leave support through her job, so she could stay at home for up to a year and I would go back to work. And I'm so glad we did. Because now that our daughter is nearly four, and our baby is one (!), I am in a place where going part-time will be far more rewarding for me, and hopefully, for my girls. Every parent is learning on the job, do it at *your* pace.

8. CONSISTENCY, NOT PERFECTION

"We all fail Mum School sometimes ... we can just start again tomorrow." – Chilli, *Bluey* Episode 14, Season 2

I could probably write a full chapter on *Bluey* as I'm sure many other parents could, but Chilli nails it—as she always does—with the above quote. Being a parent, or a working dad or mum, is not about perfection. It's about showing up. If you had to stay late at work to get a project over the line and you missed bath time, it's ok. If you haven't made it to the gym, or your diet has taken a backwards step, that's ok. Being kind to yourself and accepting that you are human and imperfect by nature, is crucial.

We are all just trying to keep those burners roaring, and those balls in the air.

RHYS MACONACHIE

MY ADVICE FOR DADS—EVEN
THOSE IN CORPORATE ROLES—IS
NOT TO FEAR BEING FLEXIBLE IN
YOUR WORK ARRANGEMENTS
OR WORRY ABOUT WHAT YOUR
EMPLOYER MAY THINK, ESPECIALLY
IF IT MEANS YOU CAN BE WITH
YOUR FAMILY IN THOSE
EARLY YEARS.

Rhys is an Executive Private Banker at Westpac and a father of three beautiful children—Sofia (four and a half), and twins Sebe and Lola (two and a half)—and happily married to Sarah, an amazing mum and the author of this book! He was born and raised in Perth, moved to Sydney for career opportunities, and came full circle, arriving back in Perth to raise his family.

RHYS MACONACHIE

AUTHOR NAME: RHYS MACONACHIE
BUSINESS NAME: WESTPAC
POSITION: EXECUTIVE PRIVATE BANKER
BUSINESS INDUSTRY: FINANCE
LINKEDIN: LINKEDIN.COM/IN/RHYS-MACONACHIE-1B450627

I was born the second of four brothers in 1987 in Perth, Western Australia. My father was a small businessman and a butcher, and my mother was a stay-at-home mum who helped with running the family business.

I would describe my upbringing, or my parents parenting style, as old-school compared to the world we live in today. But I believe it helped shape me into the person and parent I am.

Growing up, I would describe my dad as a strong father figure who had old-school values. We were taught to have respect for authority, whether it be our parents, teachers, or anyone older than us. It was expected to have good manners, strive for excellence in both school and sports, and aim to be the best in whichever path we chose. And yes, if we stepped out of line, we would certainly know about it! Interestingly, my dad didn't have his own father present during his upbringing; he only met him later in life when my siblings and I were teenagers. As a result, he was raised solely by my grandmother.

Dad worked hard from an early age and was very driven to succeed in his butcher trade. Despite referring to himself as just a 'dumb old butcher' who left school at 14, he eventually became the owner of one of Perth's largest butchering businesses. At its peak, the business had a dozen shops and a couple of business partners. This success came at a cost, with Dad working gruelling hours. He would leave home by 6:30am, return at around 6:30pm, and work Monday to Saturday. He often mentioned that he was doing all of this to provide us with opportunities he didn't have, like sending us to a private school, allowing us to participate in extracurricular activities, and go on holidays.

This left Mum to do a lot of solo parenting. She was responsible for things like school runs, after-school activities, Saturday run-arounds to whatever we were doing, and everything in between. But even though Dad was more time-poor than most other fathers, he still maximised the time he spent with us when he was home. I have very fond memories of my dad being home with us. Growing up, Dad would get home between 6:30pm-7:00pm on weekdays, and my brothers and I would argue over who was getting him his first beer. Then, as a family, we would all sit down and watch the 7:00pm ABC News and catch up before dinner. Dinner would generally involve a robust discussion, mainly myself and Dad debating the topic of the night, and then him getting frustrated with my slow eating and I'd get a form of punishment.

We were raised in what I would call the opposite of the 'cotton wool' upbringing Dad would often comment on. This meant that there was never any sugar-coating; he would call a spade a spade. So, if you had a cold, you would still be going to school (I think I only had a couple of days off the whole way through school, as you had to be on death's door to miss school). And if you got home and it was footy training, you would be on your bike down to the oval, rain, hail, or shine. We were taught from a young age that nothing in life is free, and you have to earn it. Even though our parents had the means to bring us up in relative comfort, we were put to work from the ages of 10 to 12 in the butcher shop on Saturday afternoons. We would scrub dishes or clean blood off the floor to earn some pocket money so we could buy the things we wanted—when we got older this meant saving for our first car. A strong work ethic was instilled in us from a very early age, and my brothers and I have continued this attitude throughout our careers.

Dad's advice sometimes got us into trouble. He always tried to raise us to be 'tough' and resilient, whether that meant having the courage to put your head over the footy and take a hit or, if someone in the schoolyard was giving you a hard time, rather than tell on them, stick up for yourself. It's safe to say this resulted in a couple of suspensions throughout school, but he would always have your back and tell the Dean or Principal, "That's how I've raised my sons!" At the same time, he was strict about having respect for your teachers and your peers, so if you were the one instigating and he found out, you could expect a clip around the ears or a bamboo cane when he got home.

Dad was always there to defend you or advocate on your behalf. One example I remember is from when I was in year 11 economics; I had worked really hard during the school holidays on an assignment where you were to analyse a company of your choice, and I chose Woodside Energy. As someone who wanted to be a stockbroker, I was in my element, and Dad had seen how much effort and passion I had put into this assignment. When the teacher, a strict, hard-nosed man, handed my paper back with a big F and commentary saying, "If you expect me to believe a year 11 student wrote this, you are dreaming." The next morning, Dad was at the school knocking on the teacher's door. Dad is not one to mince his words, so I wouldn't like to know what he said to my teacher, but, safe to say, my assignment was re-marked as an A with an apology. There was a remark from Mr. Wake not long after: "I don't want to have an argument with your dad again!"

Fast forward to 2019, I was 32, with mine and Sarah's first child on the way, and how my upbringing shaped the parent I wanted to be.

I would often think back to how I was raised and examine certain aspects of my upbringing. Many people might look at us being punished and think of it badly. However, upon reflection, I realised that although it may not be considered an appropriate way to treat children now, my brothers and I all turned out alright with good values, great friends, and we have all done well in our own ways.

When Sarah and I found out we would be parents, I didn't really think about it too much. There was no wondering—what does this all mean? How will we cope? Will we be good parents? Will I be a good father? How much will my life change? I feel like I just accepted this as the next chapter in life; we've got this, and I can't wait. I think it is probably a reflection of how I was raised, where you just get on with things. It might be tough, but you will get through it. This probably also reflects my wife, who was not only someone completely confident about becoming a mother, but also someone who just gets on with things.

The first decision we made about parenting was the type of lifestyle and environment in which we wanted to raise our children. At the time, we were living in Bondi, Sydney. I am from Perth, and Sarah is from England. Despite enjoying the vibrant lifestyle, pubs, restaurants, and career opportunities that Sydney offered, we, being young and carefree, realised that the hustle and bustle of a big city might not be what we wanted for this next chapter. Moreover, the exorbitant house prices would mean living in a shoebox. We wanted to have a spacious backyard for the kids to run around, be able to drive (and park) at the beach, and the support of family in the same city. So, we made the decision to move back to Perth. Only one week after I was accepted for a new role in the Perth office, Sarah found out she was pregnant.

We had a relatively smooth pregnancy, and our daughter, Sofia, entered this world happy and healthy. Initially, I had a simple mindset about parenting; show your children lots of love, be there for them, and aim to raise them as fine citizens of the world. So, it was a matter of rolling with it and finding our way, not overthinking it and adapting to challenges as they inevitably arise. Luckily, Sofia, for the most part, was an easy baby, and we didn't encounter many issues.

In 2020, with the onset of COVID, there was a significant shift in both work and our approach to parenting. Sarah became pregnant shortly after Sofia's first birthday. The real surprise came during the first scan at eight weeks. Due to COVID restrictions, Sofia wasn't allowed to accompany us to the scan, so we went back to the car and waited together. Half an hour later, I saw Sarah walking to the car in tears through the rear-view mirror. I immediately thought there was bad news, but when she opened the door in tears, she said, "Don't worry, everything is ok, but we are having twins. What are we going to do?!" I realised I had to step up. Sarah was very nervous about carrying two babies, and it wasn't the time for me to have a meltdown, so I kept it together and tried to stay positive for her.

Sarah's pregnancy went mostly well, except for the discomfort in the later stages of carrying two babies. She was understandably exhausted and struggled to pick up Sofia towards the end. So, I started working from home more to be there to help. On Australia Day 2021, Sebe and Lola were born. This was when I really started to think about what parenting looked like and how we were going to do this. One child was a breeze, but three kids under two?! How the hell are we going to juggle this? Fortunately, Westpac is a larger organisation, and has lots of parent-friendly policies. As Sarah had a C-Section, I was able to take six weeks of carers leave to help while Sarah recovered, as well as having three weeks of paternity leave. This helped a lot, giving us time to get into a rhythm and figure out how to juggle two babies at once with a toddler as well. With Sofia, my six weeks involved a holiday down south, lots of visitors, and some great days out. It was quite different the second time around. We agreed it would never be sustainable for Sarah to physically breastfeed both otherwise

WORKING DADS AND BALANCING ACTS

she would never sleep. So, she would pump milk, and we would both feed the twins together, which worked for us. Although I was probably glazed over with tiredness at work for the best part of a year, I managed to get through it.

My biggest fear was once back at work, what would this mean for me, being a man/dad doing my job, while being able to support my wife through her own work/life balance? I think COVID and the changes this caused across workplaces saved me big time. If that had never happened, I would have returned to work where the expectation would be you are in at 8:30am and don't leave before 5:00pm. If you left any earlier, you would feel guilty or fear, "Will this affect my bonus or how I am viewed?" Luckily, we had to work from home for quite a long time. So, for the first six months (I think), I was home and there for support if Sarah needed it. Once we could return to the office, I was very keen to go back in. I love the environment versus working from home, so once allowed, I was back to five days a week in the office. But with everyone working on different arrangements, I felt a lot more comfortable leaving work at 4:00pm to do daycare pick-up or help with dinners to give Sarah a break and spend some time with them all.

This relaxed mindset around flexible working arrangements was iterated when Westpac launched new benefits to recognise working dads and paternity leave, which happened around the time the twins were born. Instead of having to take your three weeks leave in the first year, you had two years to take it. Likewise, if you were going to be the primary caregiver, you could take three months. They recognised that mums usually take the first year off, and dads don't always get that opportunity. They also gave you a two-year window to take three months off as well if your partner was back at work full-time. My biggest regret is that I didn't utilise these three months of leave when I could have. As it was new, I still subconsciously thought, "How will this be viewed by leaders? Will this affect my progression or bonus?" Since then, a number of colleagues who have become dads have utilised these benefits, and I have seen that it is now accepted as a normal thing for dads to do. My advice for dads—even those in corporate roles—is not to fear being flexible in your work arrangements or worry about what your employer may think, especially if it means you can be with your family in those early years. Don't have the expectation that since you are working, it is on your wife or partner to do the heavy lifting at home. Plus, in those younger years, it is great to be able to get home and have dinner with the kids or pick them up from daycare where you can have some valuable time with them. I have a great relationship with our children and feel as though Sarah and I have a great balance in terms of sharing the load.

Fast forward to now: Sofia is four and a half, and Sebe and Lola are two and a half. And how is my 'daddying' going? I feel that we navigated and managed those early years quite well. We are probably now just getting through the toughest part with the twins going through the toddler phase. I sense that my patience is thinner, and I've leaned in more towards the strict and disciplined parenting style I was brought up with. Sarah and I have to remind ourselves often (mainly Sarah reminding me!) that they are toddlers, and they are only just learning about listening and following instructions. I try to be patient, opting to reason with them and communicate about what they've done before resorting to shouting and reprimanding, but as I realise I had very little of this in my own upbringing, it can be challenging at times. Many people looking into our house might think it's absolute chaos; the twins have a lot of energy, something parents of twins can understand! For all dads, especially twin dads, strap yourself in and support your partner. Not only does it allow your partner to follow her own dreams and desires in life, but being involved in your children's lives is the best, and I am so grateful for the relationships I have with my three.

PETER BENNETT

PRIORITISE YOUR FAMILY. SCHOOL DROP-OFFS, SPORTS CARNIVALS, TAKING YOUR MUM TO THE HOSPITAL. ALL THOSE SORTS OF THINGS ARE IMPORTANT, SO MAKE SURE YOU DO IT.

Peter Bennett is the chief executive and managing director of Clough and has more than 30 years' experience in the energy and infrastructure contracting service industry. Peter is also the Chair of CEO's for Gender Equity. Over Peter's six years as Clough's CEO, he has championed and supported the implementation of a range of initiatives to achieve both a more diverse and inclusive workplace, and a more equitable engineering and construction industry. Some of these initiatives include flexible work practices, new and updated parental leave entitlements, learning and development programs, mentoring, and leadership training for women in the business making Clough a recipient of the Employer of Choice citation by Workplace for Gender Equity Agency since 2020.

PETER BENNETT

NAME: PETER BENNETT
ROLE: CEO
COMPANY: CLOUGH
LINKEDIN: WWW.LINKEDIN.COM/IN/PETER-BENNETT-9967846/

SARAH:
Can you just start off by telling me a little bit about your own upbringing and your family as well.

PETER:
I grew up in country New South Wales as the eldest of three boys. My father always worked but my mother stopped working when I was born. So up until that point she'd also been working, but she stopped and looked after myself and my brothers. Once my youngest brother was at school, she started her own floristry business.

SARAH:
Great. And your own family?

PETER:
The same. So, we've got a boy and a girl. Grace is 15, and Jackson is 13. Juliet—my wife—also stopped working when Grace was born. The original plan was for her to go back to the workforce pretty soon thereafter, but she really enjoyed being a mum. So, she had planned to go back after a few years. Then, our son was

diagnosed with type one diabetes, so she stayed home to focus on getting that under control, getting comfortable with the school's management of his T1 and everything. She's started to go back to work now.

SARAH:
When your children were born, did you take time off? Or how did that work?

PETER:
No, I worked at that time for an American company, so the concept of parental leave was a bit foreign. I took a couple of days off around the birth, obviously, but not much more than that.

SARAH:
How did your wife cope with that?

PETER:
She's more capable and confident than I am, so she coped pretty well. I stayed local – I didn't travel for a few weeks around that time, obviously. And our daughter was born in Holland. It has a really unique program called Kramsorg. You're assigned a Kramsorg nurse (which is halfway between a midwife and a nurse) when you are first confirmed you're pregnant, and that person kind of stays with you all through the pregnancy. Then, when you leave the hospital, they basically come to your house that afternoon.

So, you get a lot of home help, and their whole concept is they will help. They'll make sure that you and your partner bond with the baby, so they help you with any kind of baby-raising queries. Also, they will cook, clean, and make the meals. It's really an impressive system. They have all sorts of aids, supports, temporary legs to lift the bed so that you're not bending over to change the baby. Really quite fantastic, very impressive.

SARAH:

Wow. I've not heard of that before – it sounds so incredible.

PETER:

Yeah, it really is. And it's available to anyone who gives birth in the Netherlands. At that time Juliet was an American citizen and I was an Australian citizen, and we were still provided that support. So that was pretty cool.

SARAH:

Amazing. I assume you wouldn't have had any family locally during that time?

PETER:

No, that was the other thing. In fact, Jackson was also born overseas in Dubai, so both times the kids were born a long way from family. With Grace, we kind of put a bit of a four-week no-visitation period because we just wanted to do that on our own rather than have people telling Juliet what she's doing wrong all the time. So no, we didn't have that. We've never had family nearby, which is not ideal, but one of the trade-offs.

SARAH:

Thanks, Peter. Now in terms of Clough, I really want talk about that a little bit with you as well.

PETER:

Well, going back to the premises of why we made some of those changes. Clough is close to 104 years old, and it has had to evolve and continues to evolve to be relevant. And, you know, we want to be not just an employer of choice, but to be able to attract good people to the business and to retain the talent that we have. We're always trying to look to see how we can improve that. I had heard some horror stories in other organisations about some of the things that returning mums were having to deal with, like expressing milk in the car park under the cover of a blanket because there were no facilities in the office, you know, just pretty fundamental things. We started to look at our own HR programs and policies but found that it wasn't very progressive. We started looking at things to help in that space, and look, everybody's different, right? But it was almost like the previous perspective followed was "if we do this, somebody will take advantage of it". Therefore, we have to make our policies so prescriptive and so tight that nobody can, right? Things like "you have to have worked for us for a minimum of 12 months before you're eligible for parental leave". It only applies to white-collar, not blue-collar. And all these thresholds, you know, assumed that flexible working is not paid childcare. Well actually it should be, right? Because childcare in this country is outrageously expensive it prohibits people from re-joining the workforce. So, we started with some of those sorts of things. What is it that we can do to help facilitate parental leave? Obviously expanding it out to both males and female. I think I mentioned when I joined the business, we had never, ever had a male take parental leave ever in the history of the business. Now it's slightly more than 50/50, with more men as opposed to women taking the parental leave. So that's been progress.

SARAH:
Amazing Peter, what an achievement, and that's in a really short period of time as well.

PETER:
Yes, and look, it comes through just messaging it right and having people that are leading loudly type of scenario. It's not about letting people take it and not tell anybody, but really promoting those sorts of successes, and that's been really quite positive. We learned a lot from engaging with those, particularly the females,

who had taken parental leave and what their experience was like, both during parental leave and upon their return.

One of them was a simple stay-in-touch program. So, you know, one of my young colleagues came back and said it was really quite frustrating because in the HR policy it says this and then something else says something contradictory, and I guess the point is, you know, they're all policies, and sometimes they just need to be torn up and started again.

But in our HR documentation, the part she couldn't get over was the fact that if you went on parental leave, you had to turn in your company phone, your company computer, email was cancelled, right? And basically give up your connection with the business while you are on parental leave. And that's obviously wrong. So we instituted, based on the discussions we had with her, a kind of a stay-in-touch program. So you get to describe how you'd like to be accessible through your parental leave period. And you decide. Do you want to just give all your stuff back and not hear from us until you're back? Do you want to get copied on announcements and different things? Do you want to have full access and visibility? Up to you. And if you change your mind after a week, month, also that's up to you, right? So yeah, pretty simple stuff to do and pretty easy from our side.

Some of these things are obvious when you become aware of it, but sometimes you need someone else to make you aware. Another employee, for example, brought up the data around the disparity in superannuation entitlements upon retirement. Right? Because when you step out of the workforce for parental leave, all that stuff stops. So, that's one of the changes we made. We now fund those superannuation contributions even when you're not in the paid period of parental leave, but at least those superannuation contributions continue so that you don't lose that continuity.

SARAH:
That's so good, you don't have that big dip that most women have.

PETER:

Exactly. And again, when you do the calculations around it, you know, what does that actually represent in terms of cost to the company? It's pretty insignificant. You look at the amount of money we waste on other ridiculous things.

SARAH:

Yeah, if you retain people you're getting that money anyway, because the amount that you probably give out in superannuation during a parental period would be less that if you had replace that position, recruitment fees, training and stuff, it costs a lot more.

PETER:

Initially, historically, you had to have worked for the company for at least 12 consecutive months. To be eligible you had to be white-collar, not blue-collar, blah, blah, blah. We took all that stuff away. Now, from the day you start, if you're pregnant or eight months pregnant on the day that you join the company, you're still eligible for parental leave, and whether you're blue-collar or white-collar, it doesn't really matter.

You know, if you look at the number of people that take parental leave each year, it's fractions of the total employee base. So, from a perspective standpoint, it's not hugely significant to the business, but in terms of creating the sort of culture that we want in the business, it has a pretty significant effect.

SARAH:

Yeah. And in terms of the way that you work, obviously your children are still in their teens and probably still need your support, but do you work flexibly yourself? Or how do you manage your time in terms of working that balance at home?

PETER:

Yes, I do. I'm very visible of the fact. You know I'll drop my kids off at school, or I drop Jack off at the bus every morning and Grace walks to school. And I try to do at least one pick-up a week. And obviously, if there's any kind of carnivals, or anything else, I attend those as well, and encourage other people to, too.

SARAH:
Well, it's a good example to set, isn't it? If you're encouraging that across the business.

PETER:
Yeah, it is. And we do. We see a good uptake in that. And there's no stigma associated with that anymore, which is also encouraging, right? So, you know, I remember at the time I joined the business, the mindset was, "I expect you to be available 24/7," and the culture was that you must be at work before your boss arrives, and leave after he goes home, sort of thing, and that's not the way anybody should work, right? You shouldn't. Yes, you work odd hours when it's appropriate for business. But it shouldn't be your normal course of business. One of my early communications to the business was exactly that.

Prioritise your family. School drop-offs, sports carnivals, taking your mum to the hospital. All those sorts of things are important, so make sure you do it. And it was interesting, the feedback that I got from people. There were a couple of people that said it got them in trouble with their wives because now they've got no excuse to not do it, which was exactly the point. But sending that communication and then visibly being seen to follow those principles myself, I think was probably a large part of what allowed that to take hold.

SARAH:
Yeah. And what would you say the biggest challenges have been from a personal perspective and a business perspective in terms

of being a working dad, and the balance between work and being a parent?

PETER:
Yeah, look, in my role, I must travel and I'm away quite a bit, but I always try to maximise my time at home. So, I would rather have dinner at home, put the kids to bed then take the midnight flight out and try to minimise the time that I'm away. I try as best as I can to schedule things so that I'm always home on the weekends. Last weekend it wasn't possible though, as we had a 50-year anniversary celebration for our Brisbane office on a Friday evening, and there was no flight home post that event. Sometimes it's unavoidable, but wherever I can, I try to schedule so I'm home as much as possible. And when I'm at home, I'll always make sure that I take the kids to school and do those sorts of things and try to maximise my time with them, and of course, with Juliet as well.

But that's probably the biggest challenge, the travel. I do pretty well about making sure that when I go home, I'm at home. Getting home, NOT opening up my laptop, and keep on working. That's not the point. I make sure that I'm home for dinner and be at home with the kids and not thinking about work. Again, sometimes there are reasons to work odd hours, and obviously we do what we need to, but it should be the exception, not the norm.

SARAH:
I think it's having that balance and being ok with it happening here and there. But you know the priority, as you said, being your family and making sure that you have that balance between what you need to be doing for work.

PETER:
Do what you need to do at home to focus on the family. Because I typically get up early, and my family typically doesn't, I can use that time to check if there are any urgent emails or anything that

needs responding to. But this was another thing that took a little while to train my team to do. If you're going to email me or call me on the weekends about insignificant things, I'm just not going to respond until Monday. Don't waste my time, don't waste your time, you know. If it's important, ok. But if it's not, don't bother me. And people do appreciate that. In my time in Holland, I learned that the Dutch have a really good work-life balance. They work hard through their work hours, and come 4:30pm, it's knock-off time and they just go home. You see a strong sense of family there, with families out walking on the beach in the evening, or out socialising... They have a really strong social fabric and it feels like they just have that work-life balance figured out and I admired that.

SARAH:
Yes – totally! So, Peter, if you were to offer some advice to working dads out there, what would it be?

PETER:
It would probably be exactly that, to really focus on your work-life balance, and when you're with the family, be with the family 100%, when you're at work, be at work. But really, proactively manage that balance.

It's not an easy thing to do; it's a juggle, right? It's a compromise, I think. But at the end of the day, you know you can work a lot of hours. But, and you know what it's like, when you work those hours, you get fatigued, your productivity drops off, and you start making mistakes. It just doesn't help anyone being in the office 12 hours a day.

SARAH:
There's not many people that can concentrate for that period of time.

PETER:

True, and it's a bit like with the working-from-home thing; we don't prescribe working-from-home rules to our people. Basically, the concept is you design what works for you, and then, as long as you and your line manager can work out what your weekly deliverables or KPIs are, it shouldn't matter when you do it, right? So design something that works for you personally. And that's ultimately the goal. There's no point saying that we want you in the office between these hours on these days as a minimum. That's not really that flexible. That's just optional, right? We've had a positive uptake around flexible work with men nearing their retirement age, young single women, and everyone in between. So, it's an interesting approach, and we've gained some really good employees that we've been able to bring back into the industry because they can design their own work program. Some had previously felt like they were unable to rejoin the workforce because being a single mum with children, time commitments are tough to juggle. We can work with these commitments and provide the flexibility to allow them back into the workforce.

SARAH:

Yeah, and that's the thing, it's being able to really—as you said—design what works for you, and be with an organisation that is able to deliver that for men and women, because it's not just about women, it's about men as well. And the important part is that the flexibility should be across both, which is great.

PETER:

Yeah, and it should be because—that is one of the things that I'll add on—is that early bonding time with your children is important, and also being there for your partner, too. That's also quite important. It's an incredible time, and a time of momentous change in your lives. Everything that used to be normal is now not and vice versa. So, it's important to have that support, for sure, and it looks different for every family, which is the beauty of it. But it's, you know, finding what it is that works for you and having the ability to do that.

SARAH:

I have to say, Peter, I just love what you've done with Clough. I think it's really inspiring for a lot of CEOs and a lot of other organisations, which is why I really wanted you to be part of this book. I really appreciate you sharing your personal journey and the incredible transformation you have created at Clough. Is there anything else you want to add?

PETER:

I think the philosophy that's kind of helped me with this and many other things is realising that I am not the ideas man in this business. Right? I mean, if the business was relying on me to develop our parental leave programs, our flexible work programs, our diversity programs, we would be nowhere near where we are today. I guess, being open-minded enough to go out and ask others within the organisation, and listening to people's needs is some strong advice.

What is difficult is knowing what could be better and just being open to change is probably the key. I'm blessed with working with some really fabulous people, and we've got a good culture to where people can bring those things up. It's been easy because we've got great people AND the culture to allow us to do that. Previously, we had some people in the business that weren't open to change. We tried so very hard to move them into the right space but just couldn't, and so ultimately, they had to move on.

SARAH:

Yeah. And I think that it's really important to acknowledge that as well. When you want to make changes and create a certain culture within your organisation. Not everybody will suit that new culture. So, being brave enough to call that out and say, "This isn't going to work for us," is a great step in the right direction, because it means that you're really passionate about what it is that you want to create and you need the right people to be able to do that.

PETER:
Yeah, you do. And that's the thing I'm very lucky with. We've got a really good team, and a lot of like-minded people, both males and females, in the business. So those sorts of changes have never had difficulty being implemented as everyone is onboard and assists with rolling things out.

SARAH:
Yeah, amazing. Well, Peter, thank you very much. I really appreciate your time.

CHRIS LLOYD

" WE DADS WILL MAKE MISTAKES;
WE ARE ALL HUMAN, WE ARE ALL
IMPERFECT, BUT WE ARE DOING
OUR BEST IN MANAGING WHAT
WE WERE TAUGHT IT WOULD BE
AND WHAT IT REALLY IS. BECAUSE
OF THAT, WE SHOULD BE KIND TO
OURSELVES AND EACH OTHER. "

Chris is a seasoned professional in Talent Acquisition with experience with ASX top 10 and NYSE, S&P 100 companies. He currently leads cross-functional project teams to develop innovative solutions for the future of work and is a founding partner of The Talent Collective, a local industry networking group that regularly connects to discuss emerging trends and workshop solutions. He is a devoted father to three children, one of whom is neurodiverse. His story provides insight into the challenges he has faced while balancing his sense of commitment to both work and his family.

CHRIS LLOYD

AUTHOR NAME:CHRIS LLOYD
POSITION: MANAGER/CONSULTANT
BUSINESS INDUSTRY: TALENT ACQUISITION
LINKEDIN: LINKEDIN.COM/IN/CHRIS-LLOYD-949A137

In October 2017, just six days before his seventy-sixth birthday, my father passed away after a gruelling battle with cancer. While we had time to prepare for his departure, the void he left behind was immeasurable.

Growing up in the industrial northwest of England during Thatcher's 1980s, I witnessed firsthand the sacrifices my father had made to provide for his family amid redundancies and layoffs. He worked tirelessly when I was young to ensure his children had food, clothing, health, and education. I played in job centres with my sister while he sought employment, he waved me off to school in the morning as he worked night shifts, and I accompanied him to the newsagents to get the weekly papers with job advertisements.

My mother was equally hardworking, balancing a full-time career in the national health service during the week with managing home affairs. Amid family outings and activities, my parents' weekend chores were unofficially separated by the door to the house. My father's domain would be maintaining the garden or fixing the car, while my mother took care of ironing, washing, or making Sunday lunch. School assemblies, sports days, and drop-offs were always handled by my mum. This was not due to anything other than my dad having to work late or do early shifts, which often saw him leave at 5:00am each morning and return 13 hours later.

Despite their hardworking ethic, my sister and I never went wanting. If there were items we couldn't afford, we were encouraged to work for them ourselves through household chores for pocket money and later by getting a job as the local paperboy or washing pots at a restaurant. It was this upbringing that taught me that a comfortable life is intrinsically linked with hard work, to never be complacent or rest on your laurels, and to always be self-sufficient and independent.

Throughout my life, my father was a guiding light, whether it was during our chats and advice sessions while kicking a ball around after he got home from work or his sense of fun on the many holidays we were fortunate to experience. He served as my confidant, offering guidance and support when my peers couldn't. Even after a gruelling day at work, he always had time for his children and created happy and lasting memories. He instilled in me the values of his generation: the importance of supporting one's family by earning a living, being a leader, and embodying chivalry and decency. His departure not only left me with a profound sense of loneliness but also a sense of anxiety. The legacy he left behind as a father and the leader of his family were big shoes to fill, and I wanted to be the best I could be for my own family.

Five years prior to his death, I had the privilege of becoming a father for the first time. It was a role I had been longing to play. When I heard my son's heartbeat on the ultrasound for the first time, it was an awakening. My wife and I had created this tiny life that was dependent on us. It gave me a stronger sense of purpose. It reset so many priorities in a matter of seconds. Maybe it's my stiff upper-lip English upbringing that means I don't cry too often, but I'm not ashamed to admit I cried that day.

The lead-up to our son's birth came with its fair share of happy and stressful moments. Diagnosed with placenta previa, my wife required a C-section for our miracle to be born. While I wasn't carrying my son for the nine months, it was important to me that I was there for both of them as much as I possibly could be. I made sure to attend every consultant meeting, every class, every ultrasound, and, of course, the surgery itself. It would be a lie not to admit that being there wasn't stressful. Many occasions were spent glancing at the clock, knowing the expectation on me to be back at work by a certain time to meet deadlines. Nevertheless, I made the appointments just the same.

When our son was born, I realised that parenthood is much more challenging and rewarding than I ever anticipated. Like stepping into a new role and discovering an ever-growing list of responsibilities and opportunities, becoming a dad can, at times, be overwhelming. The limited parental leave for fathers during the birth of my eldest child created challenges for my wife and I as a couple. Still relatively immobile from her C-section and with a back injury, the two weeks of leave entitlement offered to me at the time were simply insufficient.

Unable to be her usual active self and being thousands of miles away from any close family support whilst I was working, my wife suffered a great deal of cabin fever and depression in those weeks immediately following our son's birth. She needed me home more than my work could allow, and for the first time, I was torn in what being a good dad, partner, and 'man of the house' should be. How could I fulfill the role of a 'provider' if I removed myself from my work? I had taken on a demanding role with long hours but higher pay, adhering to the traditional male breadwinner role. Balancing that with where I should have been became a delicate juggling act that I couldn't always get right.

At work I was thinking about family and taking calls from home, and while at home, I was thinking of my job and taking calls from my employer. I was always present physically, but never in mind.

Relieving my wife from a full day of child duties after a 12-hour slog was hard. The 1980s kids' manual of being a good father and supportive husband never included anything beyond "work hard," "be a breadwinner," and "take care of the DIY." My wife also had her own career ambitions that she wanted to return to. A driven and motivated woman, she was always very clear that the stay-at-home mum life was not something that appealed to her.

My dedication to work had set us up so well before kids, but now it seemed to be working against the best interests of my family. Something had to give, and so I chose family. Within our son's first nine months, I seized a new opportunity that offered me greater working flexibility around family. I grabbed it with both hands. The flexibility provided by my new employer made our lives instantly easier, and three years later, fuelled with confidence in the success story we had created through compromise, we were excited about another new arrival and building our happy little family.

In the quiet of our home, our new baby brought new and quite different challenges. From the very beginning, he defied all expectations set by his brother: his cries pierced the night for hours, his sleep was a chaotic dance of irregular patterns, and he would awaken at random times, refusing to rest until I paced in figures of eight around our living room. Days bled into nights as we juggled the demands of a restless child. Since our first child, times had changed. After taking the benefit of a full month of secondary caregiver leave, I found myself caught in a relentless cycle: working all day, returning home to relieve my wife at night, cradling our baby to sleep in the small hours, only to wake up and do it all over again. There would be no 5:00am departures to work for me! Hints that our youngest son perceived the world through a different lens began to surface. Like any concerned parents, we followed conventional paths, making countless visits to doctors. We witnessed the removal of adenoids and made many attempts to decipher his behaviour over the years. Finally, at the age of four, we were able to secure an assessment for Global Developmental Delay and Autism Spectrum Disorder (ASD).

The diagnosis, though daunting, brought a sense of relief as it explained the quirks, meltdowns, and unique social rituals that were part of his world. It meant that we could start planning a journey that would provide him, and us, with the support and understanding he needed to flourish. Despite the early diagnosis, the application processes to secure funding for his support were long and arduous. My employer was incredibly supportive, providing flexibility during that period as I needed to take time away to attend the many appointments with my son.

My wife, having returned to work herself, simply didn't have the working flexibility to take him to the various consultations and specialist appointments. The sacrifices she made to her own career from the years spent on maternity leave far outweighed my own. Through my ability to flex work around his appointments, I was given the space to realise that my role as a dad and husband can be best served by simply being there for the family and becoming more meaningful by stepping forward to lead in other areas. I made another choice. I negotiated with my employer to work part-time in my role. My wife was eager to pursue her career aspirations after another year out of the workforce. Combined with the stress of raising a child with autism, it was challenging to find balance, and opting for part-time work felt like the solution we needed for our family.

The decision was not without its challenges. On my days "off," work continued to haunt me relentlessly. The temptation to put in extra hours, to check emails persisted. As I interacted with my baby son, I had to resist the feeling that I was somehow failing in the role society expected of me as the main breadwinner and provider. No one was telling me this; it was an internal battle with my own expectations. While I was spending time with my children, I felt like I was losing my identity with work. Overcoming that was hard, but I found that I could replace my sense of a lost identity from work with working toward the identity I really wanted— being the best dad for my kids and being present in their lives. I signed up to coach my eldest son's sports teams, used my days off to get involved in school committees, volunteered at sports day events, and handled pick-ups. I started to focus more on being a good dad and stopped seeing work as the sole means to achieve it.

Many years ago, when discussing children, my wife and I had always agreed that three was the magic number we wanted. In 2019, we were blessed with the arrival of a beautiful baby girl. The positive pregnancy news landed a few weeks after my father passed, making the news both happy and sad. Our third time was a charm; our daughter is a confident, bubbly, energetic bundle of joy who keeps us all in check. She toilet trained herself in a matter of weeks and puts herself to bed! While she can be feisty at times, her independence, determination, and confidence are attributes my wife and I encourage as traits that will serve her well as she grows up in a world that still portrays the ideal woman to be quiet and agreeable.

So, where are we today?

Now that our youngest is five and our oldest is ten, life has got easier.

My wife and I have both returned to full-time work. We still require a level of flexibility from our employers, as well as from each other, as we share the pick-ups and drop-offs between us. At home, it is important to me that my children see their dad doing the cleaning, the dishes, and laundry as much as they see him in the garden, with the car, or handling DIY. The door that once unofficially separated these duties for my parents is well and truly down in our home.

My eldest son is excelling at school; he is a polite, smart kid who has chosen a good group of friends. We share a love of soccer, and I enjoy practicing with him as much as my old man did with me. Our youngest son has come a long way since that first challenging year. Now, equipped with the right support, he is keeping up with his classmates. He still has his social quirks, but my wife and I have become much better at managing them. We've established a good support network of local friends with children the same age who lean in and support us when distant family cannot.

Despite the happy ending, you could be forgiven for thinking that my experience has been presented in a negative light. I promise you that it's not! I have loved being a dad since that first ultrasound. I share the pain points and challenges because they are true! Being a working dad can be a long, hard, and lonely slog, and while it does get easier along the way, you are forced to face everything you were told and assumed about yourself. To achieve our happy ending, we had to decide what we wanted to prioritise and what to compromise. The answers are different for all of us.

We dads will make mistakes; we are all human, we are all imperfect, but we are doing our best in managing what we were taught it would be and what it really is. Because of that, we should be kind to ourselves and each other. It's unrealistic to expect work to be completely deprioritised, but it is okay to reassess its ranking based on the chapter of life you find yourself in. Like a room of spinning plates, or a juggling of many things, there are times when you have to choose which object must fall. For me, it was my commitment to climbing the corporate ladder. Don't get me wrong, I still work hard, but I now ask myself: What choices will I regret? What memories will I cherish? How do I want my children to feel about their dad? And am I role modelling the type of parent I would like my children to be? I'm rewarded with priceless memories; the hugs at bedtime, the smiles when I do come home from being out, the Father's Day pictures and gifts they bring home and cheerfully pull out of their bags to show me. These are the things that sit on my desk and motivate me now, not the title or the paycheque.

As a boy who saw his own father make it look so simple, I have worked hard to achieve anywhere near the same. I have taken a different approach than that of my dad but come to accept that neither is worse or better; they are just different roles in different eras. The flexible working arrangements available to working dads today are significantly better than those offered to my own father and even to me in the early years of being a parent. On reflection, I realised that what I appreciated from my dad wasn't just the hard work or time spent fixing our car or maintaining our garden. It was the time that he was still able and willing to create for my sister and me.

A few weeks before he passed, I got over to the UK to see him. He'd finished his last round of chemo and I'd flown over with my eldest son to give him a much-needed morale boost. He lived for his kids and that love naturally extended to his grandkids. Driving him home one afternoon, we got talking about everything and anything, just like all those years ago when kicking a ball around after work. In that car ride he offered me his final piece of advice, "Son, just focus on your family and make sure you do right by them, the rest will either fall into place or it just isn't worth worrying about."

That is the mantra I try to live by today.

Miss you, Dad.

ROB SCOTT

" I BELIEVE, IN GENERAL, THAT IT'S THE DAD'S JOB TO 'EAT LAST,' AND TO STAY CALM AND QUIET WHEN OTHERS ARE UPSET. LET YOUR PARENTING AND HUSBAND-ING INFLUENCE BE FELT, NOT HEARD. THIS IS NOT EASY AND TAKES PRACTICE. "

As a medical professional, devoted husband, and father to two amazing kids, Dr. Robert Scott brings a unique blend of expertise and personal experience to parenting. Amidst the challenges of a medical career in Queensland, Australia, Rob finds balance and adventure in mountain biking and adventure racing. Despite his best efforts, Rob's kids still see him as a very "uncool" dad attempting to share the thrill of outdoor adventures with them. Rob hopes to inspire other dads to try to convince their kids that they are, indeed, cool – or, at the very least, interesting and funny!

ROB SCOTT

AUTHOR NAME: DR. ROBERT SCOTT
POSITION: GP, PI AND UNI SC AND NON-EXECUTIVE DIRECTOR
OF LEA
LINKEDIN: LINKEDIN.COM/IN/DR-ROB-SCOTT-2A738B37

My mum and dad loved adventures, so, for a while, we lived in a caravan as we drove from Melbourne northward, eventually settling in Bargara Beach. While I strangely hardly remember the locations we visited, I vividly recall the sense of togetherness during that journey. This lifestyle also meant that I grew up all over the place!

My father, a gentle soul, was always joking around and rarely raised his voice. As a boy, I observed his contentment in simply pushing cars back and forth with me. As a young man, I cherished hours of kicking a footy and playing cricket in the backyard. In my teenage years, I marvelled as he effortlessly soothed fussy infants and younger cousins, promptly relieving tired parents and engaging with children. He would talk to children as if they were fully functioning adults, discussing the weather, the colour of trees, and sporting events – the babies would look at this man, with his soft reassuring tone who treated them like equals, and stop crying. Occasionally, he would sit with them and, with a serious face, start playing cars—not asking if they wanted to play, but just assuming. The children most often accepted the assumption and engaged, happily playing with my dad while their tired parents relaxed back in the chair.

As an adult with my own children, I now understand the look of relief from those parents! My dad inspired me to be that same kind and gentle father who I aspire to be, but often fall short of.

FIRST BABY

Late one night, during my final exams in Medical School after seven years of relentless learning, my heavily pregnant girlfriend gently tapped me on the shoulder, "Babe… I think my waters broke."

Fuck.

This was the start of our journey into parenthood. My beautiful, cheeky, creative, wonderful daughter entered the world on the day of my final exams. I emailed the head of school from the hospital waiting room asking if I could postpone my exam. With no response (not surprising – it was past midnight), I put my phone away and entered the birthing suite. This marked the beginning of my aim to prioritise family over work, although my hospital training made achieving 'work-life balance' a formidable challenge.

I still have the little note my wife gave me when I went off to that exam: "Good luck, Daddy!" with a silver-painted footprint from our tiny girl, Lily.

Early career doctors are expected to be in the hospital all the time, and I really mean *all the time*. Additionally, junior doctors get night shifts all the time, again *all the time*. I was rostered for nights almost constantly for nine months in my first year as a medical registrar. This meant days off were spent trying to sleep, and my wife trying to keep two young kids quiet. Quiet is not a 'mode' that little kids have. I did have time with the kids early on, but I was not the husband or dad I wanted to be. Balance was so far from our thoughts at that time. It was just 'survive'.

My relationship with my wife was certainly under pressure then. She had limited support as neither of our families were close by. While she had a good mother's group, which was fantastic, there are also pressures with those kinds of groups as well. Please don't compare children!

Now, as a full-time doctor in research and general practice, I am far enough into my career that I can design my working week around my kid's drop-offs and pick-ups, for 1-2 days a week at least. I am so privileged to now be able to do this. My daughter is 11, and my son nine, and it has taken until the last two years to have the ability to craft my job into a flexible and reasonably well-remunerative activity.

My wife has recently returned to work full-time, so the chaos has returned to our home in spades. Her career is important to her, and we both feel that working mums are incredible role models for children. I am so proud of her work ethic and career achievements. I am proud just to stand beside her as we walk through this life together. Mums are pulled in so many directions: be a great wife, an even better mum, oh, and you *can* have a full-time career. But don't neglect your friendships, and try turn up to as many social outings as you can. Also make time to exercise, or you will be cranky…

I have seen some mums have an incredible ability to foster guilt about their place in the world. My gorgeous wife can feel simultaneously guilty about the kids not being involved in enough extra-curricular activities and about not dedicating enough effort or time to her job. She's frustrated that she can't exercise enough and feels the need to have some time to herself, but also feels guilty about wanting that. Blokes, in general, seem to dip their toes less deeply into that pool. I am comfortable with the kids finding their own interests, and while I agree we should help them by signing them up for sports or clubs, I'm not going to feel guilty about what they're not doing. We are all just doing our best! Lucky for me, my wife keeps us on the straight and narrow. I really think we generally find a good balance.

ADVICE

Randomly giving advice to other dads might give the incorrect impression that I know what I'm doing or somehow have my act together. Let me dispel that notion right away. That said, I think some general principles can be universal. I believe, in general, that it's the dad's job to 'eat last,' and to stay calm and quiet when others are upset. Let your parenting and husband-ing influence be felt, not heard. This is not easy and takes practice.

Meditation has given me immense calm and an expanding, albeit still small, space between my thoughts and my voice. That tiny space is priceless. No parent wants to be snapping at their kids.

If an adult behaved in your home the way my children act, you would probably forcefully remove them, calling them sociopaths or calling the police! Try not to impose adult values on your little people. They are doing the best that they, as kids, can do. They are doing their *kid-best!*

Allow yourself a gap, count to six, take one deep breath, and exhale slowly. Then, consider how you will respond. At the very least, the vision of you closing your eyes and breathing, with your neck arteries pulsing with rage, may give the children a moment's pause to consider the best way forward!

My daughter sometimes struggles to sleep. I have taught her a 'floating on a cloud' exercise. It's basically a visualisation where I try to make my voice as calm and soothing as possible, slowly describing tranquil landscapes with reassuring tones: "You are floating beside a huge mountain with perfectly white snow and dark black rocks breaking through it. You are safe and warm on your cloud." It starts with a deep breath in through the nose and out through the mouth, trying to extend the outward breath.

Learning breathwork is another game-changing skill, whether you're a dad or not. Being able to assist those around you requires having your shit together. Take a deep breath in, hold for three seconds, and exhale slowly through pursed lips. Do that now and see how it feels. If you can learn to do that consistently, life may lean just slightly toward the calmer end.

Last week, both our kids were at a sleepover. Sorry – that is a misnomer; when there are four kids in the same room, there is little sleep! My daughter said that she tried to guide the group through 'floating on a cloud' to get them to calm down. I felt incredibly proud and validated to see some of my parenting had an impact on her!

Relationships are hard. Children make them harder. Finding the balance between both your careers, parenting, and being your own self is like asking how water flows down a stream. Its complex in its detail, but simple in principle.

If you can manage your own mind, calm your own responses, be kind and thoughtful towards your partner, make a habit of validating your partners feelings and practicing compassion and empathy, if you can delay your own gratification and goals for a little while, then you are starting to move yourself towards the idea of balance.

GEORGE ROLOGAS

"I AM A BIG BELIEVER THAT MY
CHILDREN WILL REMEMBER THE
TIMES I SPENT WITH THEM, NOT THE
THINGS I BOUGHT FOR THEM."

George Rologas, a proud father of two, is a business owner and trusted strategic advisor to SMEs in Adelaide. As a self-taught web designer, he brings a natural creative flair and a collaborative, no-nonsense approach to elevate brand presence. Specialising in crafting clean, unique, and interactive digital designs, George is dedicated to delivering high-quality solutions aligned with the client's vision. Recognising the importance of strategic opportunities, he partners transparently with businesses, demonstrating a proven ability to identify, prioritise, and guide them toward success.

GEORGE ROLOGAS

AUTHOR NAME: GEORGE ROLOGAS
BUSINESS NAME: THE BRAND SOCIETE
POSITION: FOUNDER
BUSINESS INDUSTRY: DIGITAL + SOCIAL DESIGN, BRANDING, HR
+ TALENT ACQUISITION
WEBSITE: WWW.THEBRANDSOCIETE.COM.AU
LINKEDIN: LINKEDIN.COM/IN/GEORGEROLOGASLINKEDINEXPERT

Our children model their behaviour based on what they see from us—their parents. We can try all we want to explain things to them, but they will learn through our examples, especially in times of adversity.

I think about the way I'd like my children to parent when they make me a grandfather, and my overwhelming hope is that they will be present, engaged, and happy. If that is my hope for my children, then I need to provide that example to them.

About six months before I started writing this chapter, I began writing a guide for living a happy and fulfilled life that I will eventually give to my children. Whilst I wrote it for my children, it is also a guide for me. I don't only want to teach them, I want to show them how I lead by example. I still have some work to do, and I'll share more about this at the end of this chapter.

I grew up in a broken family – my parents divorced when I was too young to remember. I mostly lived with Mum, seeing Dad on the weekend fortnightly. That was just the normal arrangement back then. I saw my mum struggle through the early years of my life trying to raise my brother and me. She managed to make ends meet, but struggled financially and sacrificed a lot to give us what we needed. I have deep respect and appreciation for what she did for us.

My dad was (is) a very loving father, and while emotional intelligence is not his strong suit, he tries his best. Both of my parents were engaged and active in my life. They were amazing role models in some ways, and not so much in other ways. There are things that I want to replicate, and others that I don't, but I have a lot of love and compassion for my parents and understand they are the way they are because of their own upbringing. That's the lens I use to approach my own parenting style. If I fast-forward to 20 years from now, I'd like my children to think of me as a role model that they will want to echo in their own personal expression as parents, and in life.

I remember my parents arguing a lot. Every pick-up and drop-off for the swap-over seemed like an argument broke out, and that has certainly shaped me as a parent. It's funny how things turn out; I am divorced myself. However, I proudly co-parent (50/50) amicably with the children's mum. We rarely argue to the extent that our nine-year-old daughter struggles to understand why we aren't together. She often says, "But you and Mummy don't even fight, so I don't understand why you can't be together." Bless her. It's interesting how our childhood experiences manifest. We can choose to let them define us or shape us. We are conditioned from a young age into patterns of behaviour and thinking that become stubborn to change or even recognise as we get older. I am privileged to be able to teach to my children the lessons I've learned through my own challenges and experiences in life.

I am very blessed to have two amazing stepparents who played significant roles in my upbringing. They embraced my brother and me as their own. My stepfather ran his own business, which afforded him a lot of flexibility and freedom. He certainly inspired me in my business pursuits. He taught me about romance, passion, emotion, and vulnerability. He provided a great life for me when he married my mum. Some of the best memories of my childhood are the times we shared together.

My stepmother is an incredibly strong woman. She taught me (and still does) about discipline, strength of character, acceptance, and will. She was the breadwinner and I've learned a lot from observing her approach to balancing work, life, and everything in between. I admire her courage and the humble way in which she lives her life.

All four parents shaped my approach to parenting.

My story of paternity leave is certainly unique. I had back surgery (which was not successful) two weeks before my daughter was born. Destiny determined that I had a long road to recovery, and I wasn't able to return to work for quite some time. I came to realise this was a blessing in disguise. The children's mum returned to work about six months after giving birth, and I took on the role of stay-at-home dad. It was an incredibly difficult period of life for my family and I at the time, but one I look back on with gratitude for the time I was able to spend with my daughter, for the amazing support we received from family and friends, and how I grew as a person. While I was experiencing pain and unable to work, my daughter was a blessing and a source of purpose – she taught me how to be present.

For the last 4-5 years, I've run my own consulting business (just myself), providing a lot of flexibility to be engaged and present with my children as much as possible. I am a big believer that my children will remember the times I spent with them, not the things I bought for them. My time and energy are the greatest gifts I can give them. I can't imagine working in a traditional 9-5 job and doing what I currently do with my kids. I have my children one week on, one week off, so I structure my work around that. During the weeks I don't have them, I play catch-up with work, so when I do have them, my focus is 100% on them as much as possible.

I drop them off to school every morning, do school pick-ups at least 2-3 times per week, and we spend quality time together on the weekends. We have dinner together six out of seven nights. I put them to bed every night. I take an interest in their passions and listen just to listen. I allow my children the space to express themselves and feel heard without judgment.

It takes a village to raise a family, and I am very grateful for the support I have from my parents who help me juggle it all. I've learned to become better at asking for help. No one can do it all on their own, and we, as parents, need to be kind to ourselves. I see too many parents these days succumbing to the expectations of society, feeling like they need to attend every assembly, every school event, every sporting event, and every extracurricular activity, whether it's morning or night. The pressure to host over-the-top birthday parties and the general expectations we put on ourselves are often more about how we want other people to see us as parents rather than what is best for us and our families. Don't worry – I have been that parent.

I had a recent experience that reinforced my evolving way of thinking. My six-year-old son has ASD (autism spectrum disorder) and becomes triggered at public events where he is performing an activity or is the centre of attention. This extends across sports, school, and other events. If too many people he knows, especially family members, are watching him in these environments, he experiences a lot of anxiety. Earlier this year, my son's reception class hosted a school liturgy. His class had learned songs to sing and dance. As soon as my son saw me sitting with the other parents, he started crying and ran to me. He didn't participate during the liturgy. This wasn't the first time this happened. A question came to me, "Do you want Daddy to come to these things?" He promptly replied, "NO!" Straight after the liturgy, I rang his psychotherapist and asked for her advice, which was simple: if he doesn't want you there, then don't go. My point here is that the expectations we place on ourselves as parents can cloud our perspective about what our children want and need.

It's easy to get lost in the chaos of parenting and life in general. Being present and grateful for the time I spend with my children is something we work on every day. I love being able to spend a lot of time—much more than most dads that I know—with my children in a range of contexts to observe their personalities and character unfold. We enjoy getting out into nature, which is something I think is so important for children, and experiencing things together.

As a parent, it's important that we look after ourselves so that we can be the best version for our children. I love the relationship I have with my children. I've seen how my daughter and son have shaped me as a person and a parent, something all parents need to embrace. My daughter is incredibly mature for her age. She is creative, emotionally intelligent, kind, curious, and sensitive. My daughter has taught me to see the world through the eyes of a child. I love her interpretation and expression of life, and she reminds me how easily we can lose perspective and miss what is right in front of us. She has taught me to become more in touch with my emotions and vulnerability. My son is a typical boy in many areas – he needs physical activity to regulate but also needs physical touch. He is generous, observant, inquisitive, kind, and has the best sense of humour. His confidence continues to grow. My son has taught me patience and acceptance. Since his early ASD diagnosis, the children's mum and I have put in the work to provide him with the best foundations to thrive. This has been a process of realisation, managing expectations, and embracing his unique traits. There have certainly been many challenges along the way, and moments where I have been stubborn to realities, but these are things I've come to learn (the hard way at times). My son has taught me to find the humour in any situation, to sense his energy and anticipate his needs, and to re-frame my own way of thinking to view the world through his eyes.

JOHN PARK

" ALL YOU CAN DO IS YOUR BEST AS
A PARENT, I THINK, AND IF YOU PUT
THESE GOOD VALUES INTO THEM
BY THE TIME THEY'RE SIX YEARS OLD,
THEN YOU PROBABLY GOT THEM
STARTED OFF RIGHT, AND YOU HAVE
CREATED STRONG BOUNDARIES. "

John Park is a partner at Dentons Law firm. After a successful career in the Federal police, John moved into Law and has continued in this field since. John is a father of 4 children, and leads a successful team of high performing lawyers at Dentons in the recovery and restructuring team.

JOHN PARK

NAME: JOHN PARK
ROLE: PARTNER
COMPANY: DENTONS
LINKEDIN: WWW.LINKEDIN.COM/IN/JOHN-PARK-LAWYER/

SARAH:
Can you tell me a little bit about how you were raised and your family dynamic?

JOHN:
I think it would be safe to say that it was tough love. My dad was very tough, very masculine. The kids should be seen and not heard approach, but at the same time, he was very supportive. He was supportive to the extent that, if you had an interest, he wouldn't discourage that interest.

He never had a driver's licence until he was probably in his 60s, so he wasn't able to drive anyone around or do anything. Because coming out of London, they didn't need to drive, so he didn't get one until he moved here. My poor mum did most of the driving. In our family, there were nine kids – I have six sisters and two brothers. It was a lot of work in raising nine children in a four-bedroom house. We built our own extension on the house to get two more bedrooms.

When we were young, Dad asked if we wanted a swimming pool, and we said yes. So he got some shovels and we used to come home from school, us boys—and we were probably, I want to say 12 or 13 at that time—and we used to dig a hole in the back garden until dinnertime. Dad's approach was; if you want it, you earn it.

One day we came home and there were people with a machine digging the pool, and Dad said, "You know your major effort? Now you can have a pool!" And then we still used to help and do the concrete and that sort of stuff. It brought in good life lessons. That's the style of upbringing we had.

We also did boxing since we were young – six years old. We used to box in the house with him or with each other.

SARAH:
And what about your mum? Did she work, or did she stay at home raising nine kids.

JOHN:
Mum worked tirelessly raising nine children, plus she was involved at the school. She worked in the school canteen and things like that. There are times, because of money, she would work as well as do all the cleaning or other things. She was always a volunteer and she volunteered for so many charities. And she would work making things for fetes and things like that, like knitting or crocheting. She was very community driven. She was a very, very selfless woman.

SARAH:
In terms of your upbringing and how you were raised, do you think that you've taken those traits on as a dad yourself? Or have you changed the way that you parent?

JOHN:
I sometimes catch myself with those traits. I think a lot of the traits are very positive, so I still maintain them. But what I try and do is soften the giving of those messages and the giving of those life

lessons. And I do catch myself sometimes thinking, "Is this soft enough? Or is this too hard?" I really do not want to be my dad. My dad was very 'black or white' and some of the punishments that he did were pretty harsh.

SARAH:
So, just run me through, because you've got four children?

JOHN:
Yep, I was married. That marriage didn't last, but it was very beautiful in that I had a daughter, who is now 30, and a son who is 28. And I can still remember to this day the day that Hannah was born; it was just a remarkable day. Not that I don't remember the others, but I think the first one, plus being a girl, was very memorable. I remember at the time, a friend whose family is very good friends of mine, his mum and dad both said, "This is the best thing that could happen to you having a girl first because if you had a boy first, there would be too much adventure. You wouldn't calm down."

And then I've got a 15-year-old boy and a 13-year-old boy with my current wife and they live at home with me.

SARAH:
And you're a lawyer? Which is quite a time-consuming position. Did you take time off with your wife when your children were born, or what did you do?

JOHN:
It's interesting when you reflect on these things. And it's, you know, a bit sad, in a way, seems a bit tragic, but when Claire had our first child, James, who's now 15, I was on the phone to work in the morning with something pretty important for a client. I remember because her waters broke and we were going to the hospital. No labour, no contractions or anything. When we got to the hospital we were sitting in the car parked outside, and I was on the phone. We must have

sat in the car, probably for 20 minutes. She would tell you it's a lot longer, but I think it was about 20 minutes. The ladies in the hospital told me off, which, as I thought, was all in good jest. But yeah, and I thought that Claire was just going to get sort of checked over and I would be taking her back home and then go to work. I didn't realise that this was it. Then we were, you know, staying there. My mind was probably not on caring for her as much as it was on work.

But once I was there, I was okay. I didn't do anything; I didn't even have my computer. And with the second baby, I didn't take a call or do anything; I was good. It was the early hours of the morning. I took the day off when they arrived, but then I was back in the office the next day.

SARAH:
How did Claire—and your previous wife—how did they cope with that work life? Were they okay?

JOHN:
Well, in the first instance with my first baby, I had some time off and I took leave. I was in the Federal Police at that time, and I messed that up as well in some ways because I did say I would have leave for a certain amount of time. One morning I got a phone call, and I took the call, and then those were the days when the phones were on the wall in the house. Mobile phones were still very, very large things that you had to carry around with a big antenna sticking out the top of it. So, I took the phone call. I can still remember my then-wife – her name is Stephanie, and I can remember her saying to me, "That was work, wasn't it?" And I said, "Yes," and she said, "You're going away, aren't you?" And I said yes. And I can still remember she was very disappointed that the week or two weeks, or whatever it was that I'd agreed to take, she was disappointed that they called me and she was disappointed that I said yes.

SARAH:

Do you look back and wish that you'd spent more time at home with your first born?

JOHN:

I was terrible with my first baby. I ended up putting her bassinet next to my bed and would sleep with my arm in there because I couldn't hear her breathing and would worry, so I always wanted her around. Then I learned from that, and I was better with the rest. But then we put her in the nursery and had one of those things where you could hear the sound, and we had it turned up so loud that in the end we just had to can that whole idea and just suck it up and every morning go and see if she was still okay.

Both Stephanie, Claire, and I were all very disciplined about the babies' routines, except for how I was with my first one. She was tough. She would go to bed at night-time, and she'd wake up about 10:30pm, or 11:00pm, completely fully recharged. I was a night-time person, so, I would have Hannah during those times.

SARAH:

Well, it sounds like you helped a lot, though, during the night, which is a big thing.

JOHN:

Oh, yeah, I helped where I could during the nights. But all my babies were breastfed for a reasonable period. Some needed weaning, some didn't really need weaning because they just gave it up themselves. You know, they first taste something solid and then go! Like our youngest, Liam, he just wanted food, so he cut himself off.

SARAH:

You told me a story about you coming home in the week and your boy being surprised that you were there. Are you happy to share that story? Do you know which one I'm talking about?

JOHN:

Yeah, I do, because it's sad. Both happy and sad. I was working as a lawyer then in my own practice. I worked long hours, and we were strict on our boys, our 13 and 15-year-olds. This is my baby who is now 13; he must have been four or five years old at the time.

They used to go to bed at 6:30pm, and I would get home after bedtime. I'd also go to work most days before they were up and about in the mornings. But when I got home, I'd go and see them and tuck them in or whatever.

One night, I was home a bit earlier and it was time for me to help get the boys into bed, and we were talking about bedtime and what to do, and my little one said to me, "Well, you don't live here?" And I said, "What do you mean I don't live here? I'm your dad. I live here. This is my house. It's all of us." And he said, "No. You don't live here, not like the rest of us live here. You just come some nights, and you sleep in my mum's bed, and then you go to work, and then some nights you come back. So you don't live here." And I was absolutely heartbroken. I couldn't believe it. I was shocked, hurt, I don't know… It's a very, very tough message.

Well, it was terrible. It was really, really terrible, and I love that little boy to death. But for him to have that opinion that I was really just a part-time parent and there wasn't even a question about it. The fact he didn't think I live with my family, you know, that was pretty tough. And it was probably tough for me because I didn't live with my first two from when they were sort of five and seven—or six and eight—from us breaking apart, and it was a bit fractured. Then they came and lived with me again for a while and went back to their mum again. So, it was hard.

That day I said to Claire that I wasn't going to go to work early in the mornings. This is my big give. I won't go to work in the morning until the kids are up and have gone to school, and I've pretty much stuck with that.

There are days, of course, when I haven't been able to do that

– there's always that exception. But as a general rule, I changed my behaviour that day. I'm big on not working at home. I've done work at home, and even last week I got caught out with something and I did work from home. But I've also generally taken a position not to take my work home because that's family time, and I like to keep the two separate.

SARAH:
John, you're a Partner at Denton's law firm. Is that flexibility pretty well accepted for what parents need? Especially mums and dads in terms of being able to do school pick-ups and things like that – does Denton's have that flexibility?

JOHN:
Denton's is a very good place to work for all of those types of things – it's very accepting of those propositions as a firm. How it works in individual teams would come down to how the teams work individually. The firm's culture is what you've said – very flexible and accepting of parents. I would anticipate that it is well and truly entrenched in every team. In my team there are a couple with children, and they do school drop-offs almost every day, and will go to assemblies and things like that. That's life. Claire, my wife, is in my team; she's a lawyer as well, and she's always had that ability to prioritise the kids.

SARAH:
What would you say your biggest challenges have been as a working dad?

JOHN:
You always—and maybe it's me or people of my generation—you always want to provide. You have this drive to be the provider, and you want to be recognised for that in some ways and not be taken for granted.

Therein lies the challenge that to provide as well as you can and be consistent but still find time to be fully immersed at home is the big, big challenge.

And then the second biggest challenge, I think, is wrestling with myself about being this provider but missing out on so much because of that. You miss out on a normal day. You miss out as the dad in the role that I've taken and how I've played it. I've missed out enormously in their life because I've worked consistently 50 or 60 hours a week for all of their lives. When I was in the Federal Police, I didn't work that many hours. But I worked in a job that took me away a lot. So, lots of away time, averaging over 250 days a year. It was massive, and then when that stopped I was in a more normal policing role, although, I don't think you call anything normal when you're in a policing role. It's not normal.

There were still the times when you did shift work, or you did long, long hours—they still happened—but it was much more balanced than lots of other people who do shift work. And that can actually be fantastic.

SARAH:
And if you were to give advice to other working dads or parents out there, what would you advise them?

JOHN:
I don't know if I'm qualified to give any! I think you've got to try and be present when you are there – be there in the moment, and don't be so tough on yourself, you know. If you're home, lay there with the kids and wife, and just be in that moment with them. That's what I would say is my advice. And I think we can be very tough on ourselves because you are pulled and pushed from so many different directions.

That's one thing we don't do: this half-brother, half-sister stuff. They're all brothers and sisters. We don't do 'half' anything. What you do will rub off on your children. That critical thinking rubs off on them, but at the same time, both my boys and one of their friends have criticised or critiqued me because they find it very hard to satisfy me, they think I always feel that they're not doing good enough or not trying hard enough. I want them to be the best they can be at everything and not slack off.

SARAH:
They'll thank you for it when they grow up! Is there anything else you want to add that you feel is important to share?

JOHN:
I tell my kids all the time to love their mum. I suppose I just expect it. If you've got people in your life that are very special to you, like my wife clearly is very special to me, I don't want to see my boys dealing with her in any way that does not recognise how special she is to them. Do not let me think that you're not recognising how special she is to me. It's important to appreciate the people that are around you.

And not just use them to be driven everywhere or given everything. That's the hard part when you're not around so much, making sure that they appreciate what they have. You don't want them to be necessarily entitled to it, and that's the difference, it can be taken away. Hopefully I'm instilling some sense of, you know, work ethic and common sense.

All you can do is your best as a parent, I think, and if you put these good values into them by the time they're six years old, then you probably got them started off right, and you have created strong boundaries.

They might get edgy because they got in trouble or got denied something, but if they choose and want to push, push, push – you just have to hold. That's the parenting tip. Set your boundaries and hold your boundaries. Hold them, even when they try and push it every now and then.

You've got to give them a little push back in, take their phone off, and turn off the Internet, deny them a trip to the beach that was promised. Be hard on them. They'll respect that. Everyone teaches their kids cause and effect when they're little. If you touch the hot oven, you'll get burnt. This is the basic cause and effect when they're 15, I'm still having to reinforce cause and effect.

Like, if you leave your stuff out everywhere all over your room, that will cause an effect. You'll look for your phone and it'll be gone. And miraculously, when your room's cleaned up and your bed is made, the phone might find its way back to you.

SARAH:
Yeah, it's very true, and they're very good tips. Holding boundaries can be really hard. I think it's such an important thing to hold boundaries with children as much as they push them.

JOHN:
I talk to people about the pots of life. My theory of pots of life: there's one big pot and if you keep taking stuff out of it, one day you'll put your hand in there and there will be nothing left. I talk about it to my boys often, even at the dinner table I'll say, "What have you put into the pot this week? Did you give your mum a hug today? What did you do to contribute to our life, to our family's life, to other people's lives?" And they always groan and moan about it. I've threatened them several times that I'm actually going to go and get a big pot and make them write things down and I'm going to check it. But I think they know I've bluffed that one too many times.

But I talk to them about this pot of life, and all four of my children have had to put up with my pot of life analogy, and I think it's very important. It's appreciating what they have and having gratitude about what they're doing. Creating that positive perspective is really quite good for their mental health.

SARAH:
That's brilliant and a great lesson to teach your children. I might use that myself. Thanks so much John. I really appreciate your time.

THOMAS BATCHELOR

" I THOUGHT JUST FOLLOWING
INSTRUCTIONS AND HELPING OUT
WHEN ASKED WAS ENOUGH.
DON'T GET ME WRONG – IT'S STILL
GOOD, BUT IT DOESN'T ASSIST
WITH THE MENTAL LOAD OF HOME. "

Thomas Batchelor is a proud husband and the father of two boys. While Tom states that he's not necessarily the smartest person in the room, he surrounds himself with good people and always asks the right questions. He loves hearing a story, especially from people who have had to overcome adversity. Tom is a bloke who wants to make a difference and help like-minded people achieve greatness, however that looks. His current goal is to be a more present dad who enjoys the process as much as the outcome.

THOMAS BATCHELOR

AUTHOR NAME:THOMAS BATCHELOR
BUSINESS NAME: SHELL ENERGY
POSITION: OPERATIONS & MAINTENANCE ELECTRICIAN
BUSINESS INDUSTRY: POWER GENERATION / GAS
LINKEDIN: LINKEDIN.COM/IN/THOMAS-BATCHELOR-37136456

I was raised in a loving home with my brother and sister (twins – 18 months younger). My parents are still together today, and they love each other very much. I don't remember a time when my parents argued in front of us kids. They were always on the same page when we were around and didn't get involved in our issues as we got older. We had to sort it out for ourselves. My childhood was 'stable'.

I met my then girlfriend (now wife), Rene, when I was 16 and she was 15. I finished my apprenticeship, and Rene graduated from school, then university as a lawyer. We travelled the world, purchased our first house, became proud dog owners, and got married. Things were going pretty well, so we decided to start a family.

I'm not prepared to sit here and tell you everything was amazing, because at the time it wasn't. Our first child (Oscar) was a nightmare—20 months of getting up four times per night. I took the initial four weeks off work (two weeks paternity and two weeks partner pay).

I couldn't wait to get back to work after that four-week period.

I thought my life would continue on its merry way. How wrong I was! Having the first child will always be the hardest; you long for the life you had. I truly underestimated how hard it would be.

I felt for my wife at home as she grappled with how difficult our first son was; he wouldn't settle, the smallest sound would wake him up, and he simply didn't want to sleep. She was not enjoying the experience of being a stay-at-home mother.

When Oscar was nine months old, my wife returned to work for two days a week and Oscar went to daycare on those days. At the time, we didn't know that our son has a compromised immune system. As it turns out, daycare was not an ideal place to send him, this resulted in a lot of carers leave and stress.

I work at a power station and my boss was initially understanding and sympathetic to my needs. Was it all smooth sailing? No, it wasn't. My boss couldn't understand why I needed to leave early or take time off to look after Oscar instead of my wife. There are a lot of privileges that parents have now that didn't exist seven years ago. Parental leave is more flexible and gendered stereotypes are changing.

If you speak to most women who work part-time on a salary, it's essentially a full-time workload with a part-time tagline (overtime, logging in when the kids go to bed, etc.), and this was no different for us. Rene was extremely busy, and the pressure was starting to build. She couldn't take time off every time Oscar fell sick; that responsibility fell on me as she would then fall further behind at work. It was a challenging situation.

It wasn't until I took this year off work that I was able to understand and appreciate how much the mother does. I thought just following instructions and helping out when asked was enough. Don't get me wrong – it's still good, but it doesn't assist with the mental load of home. Understanding what is required without being told is the real support. I just didn't know any different until I became the primary caregiver. It could well be a bloke thing, but I can guarantee it wasn't on purpose.

During my mid-20s, I generally thought about my wife advancing in her career while I stayed at home with the kids. I've always felt comfortable playing the support role and seeing her advance. I get just as much satisfaction from it, if not more. Having my incredible wife on the sidelines for too long would be a waste of talent. I know that with the right setup at home, women can be both amazing mothers and have successful careers. Rene is proof of this in my eyes.

We slowly recovered from the challenges of the first child after about 2.5 years, then welcomed our second child, Joshua, into the world. Joshua's birth was an enjoyable experience, and he was a good baby all in all. My wife enjoyed her 12 months of maternity leave, and things were going okay! Then, COVID-19 happened.

The lockdowns and challenges between home and work took their toll. I really struggled during this period, and COVID forced us to make some changes at home. As a couple, we decided that Rene would take 12 months off from work and return to full-time study while playing the primary caregiver role. This would also help me concentrate on work and relieve some of the home pressures. Rene finished her corporate governance qualification within those 12 months, something that generally takes three years in a part-time capacity! I don't know how she managed full-time study and being the full-time primary caregiver.

Did it slow things down for me? Yes, but if I'm honest I think she sheltered me from the challenges of home. My boys are full on and it's not enjoyable at times.

This study year led to my wife securing an executive position, and I applied for 12 months' leave without pay. Fortunately, I work for an employer that has policies around parenting and flexible work arrangements. My employer held my position for 12 months while we adjusted to the new normal, and for that, I'm grateful. Many parents would have struggled and worked tirelessly to demand these privileges; without them, it would be very different. So, thank you.

It is a credit to Shell, the HR team, and management for supporting myself and, consequently, supporting my wife. It shows they are serious about promoting women in executive roles and changing the status quo, not only for their own employees but also for their families. My 12-month leave is due to expire in January 2024, and I have successfully negotiated a two-day workweek.

The future is filled with so many fun things with my boys: weekend sports, camping trips, family holidays. I feel lucky that I am going to be so involved in shaping the men they will become and get to spend quality time with them while doing so. I am also learning and growing so much myself; it really is an honour to be on this journey.

Like lots of boys, they have a lot of energy, so keeping them entertained can be a challenge in itself! The demands that boys with lots of energy place on parents can be tough. And, of course, sibling rivalry is apparent.

My advice to dads is this: be the man you want your kids to see. Walk towards the problem, surround yourself with good people, and don't be afraid to ask for help when you need it. Raising kids is not a competition; we're all out here trying to do the best we can.

These are the things I live by: exercise daily, eat healthily, maximise sleep, drink plenty of water, stay in communication with your partner (Where am I at? Where are you at? What do I need? What do you need? What do we need?), find a men's support group, turn notifications off, and if you mess up, tomorrow is another day.

DOUGLAS VEAL

" DURING THIS TIME, MY WIFE
WAS AWAY FROM WORK FOR
NINE MONTHS, PARTLY DUE TO
NEEDING OPEN-HEART SURGERY.
NOT TO BE DRAMATIC, BUT IT WAS
A WHIRLWIND FIRST YEAR INTO
FATHERHOOD WHEN, AT TIMES, WE
CONFRONTED THE POSSIBILITY OF
ME GOING IT ALONE. "

As a seasoned leader with experience in various operating environments, including policing, State Emergency Service (SES), and the Australian Army, Douglas has developed skills in crisis management, critical reasoning, and effective communication. In 2019 he was awarded the Australian Army (Reserves) Skill at Arms Trophy, and in 2020 he was awarded the Western Australia Police Force Medal. Douglas holds postgraduate qualifications in Business Administration and Leadership and Management, and undergraduate qualifications in Human Resource Management, Public Safety, Program Management, Work Health and Safety, and Government Investigations. He is a loving husband and a devoted father.

DOUGLAS VEAL

AUTHOR NAME: DOUGLAS VEAL
BUSINESS NAME: AUSTRALIAN PUBLIC SERVICE
POSITION: ASSISTANT DIRECTOR
BUSINESS INDUSTRY: GOVERNMENT
LINKEDIN: LINKEDIN.COM/IN/DOUG-VEAL

My name is Doug. I have previously been certain of my identity; a singular definition of who I am and my place in the world. Ten years ago, it was a police officer, six years ago, a detective (and husband to my lovely wife Nicola), five years ago... well it became more complex. I became a father. Pre-fatherhood, life was relatively simple.

I had a good childhood. We weren't wealthy, but we had a very loving home. I grew up in a dynamic family environment. We fostered kids and it wasn't uncommon for me to wake up, as a seven-year-old, sharing my bedroom with a new family member. And that's what they were, it didn't matter if they were only there for the weekend or for years, they became family.

I had great role models, and I tried to emulate my brother. He studied finance and economics; I studied finance and business law. He spent months abroad, I spent years. Being away from home is something that really helped me build my character. I have spent a month or more on six of the seven continents—Antarctica eludes me, but that's another story for another time.

I got a rush from exposing myself to different environments with big challenges, such as:

- Travelling around Lesotho, South Africa, without speaking the language or having decent maps.
- Planning and completing a three-week trek to Everest basecamp, sitting at an altitude of ~5000m.
- Navigating the jungles of Rwanda to stalk mountain gorillas.
- Taking a trip along the Amazon River exploring Brazil, Peru, and Columbia without power, internet, or phones.

Putting this into a skill development context, I was learning to listen, negotiate, prioritise, and collaborate to get what needed to be done... done.

When making my way back to Australia, I organised to meet two of my sisters and my brother in India. We toured Rajasthan and made our way down to Mumbai. We went out to dinner at the Leopold Restaurant with some new friends we had made just hours before. We ordered our food and excitedly started to plan the next few days. Two men walked in with duffle bags and sat at a table nearby. They ate their food, paid, then without hesitation, took out their rifles and started shooting people. These men killed 10 people inside the restaurant that day. My siblings, new friends, and I fled on a horse-and-cart back to our hotel. The day was 26th November 2008. It was the start of the Mumbai terror attacks that cost 175 people their lives. I spent the next four days planning and preparing how to get out of the city while trying to keep my family safe. I had to be the calm in the unfolding chaos. I was able to secure passage to the airport via the British High Commission with an escort from the Indian Army and two Hilux Utes with tray-mounted machine guns.

From this point, I knew I wanted to work in that chaos, either through the emergency services or the military. I ended up doing both. I arrived home, joined the State Emergency Service, and submitted my application to join the Western Australia Police. Later, I joined the ADF (Australian Defence Force), commencing the commissioning course. As you can imagine, the world of finance had lost its lustre.

In the police, I enjoyed helping people in crisis. I became a detective early in my career and found that the best way to learn is to work in a range of portfolios. Over 12 years, I worked in nine different divisions, both regionally and in the metro area, enhancing my skillsets and learning valuable lessons from each office I worked in. My roles included a local uniformed officer, district detective, and on a state level, a detective in the:

- Major Crime division investigating unnatural deaths including homicides,
- Financial Crime division pairing up with the CCC investigating corruption within state government departments, and
- Serious and Organised Crime division investigating and disrupting the economy of transnational organised crime networks by targeting their money laundering efforts.

Yes, this was my simple life… I say that in jest, but there is a certain simplicity in having a moral direction, an overarching purpose, and a structured approach that you can share with your team to achieve a shared goal. In parenting, that team is, for the most part, you and your partner—no analyst, no clocking off, no end-of-shift handovers, or 'closing the book'.

A common expression is that women become mothers when they get pregnant, and men become fathers when their child is born. Personally, I don't subscribe to this. When Nicola was pregnant, life changed for both of us. We faced medical issues that made the pregnancy high-risk for both Nicola and our unborn child, Edison. We were in survival mode. There is little life balance when you are surviving. From 26 weeks, we had appointments every Tuesday to see if we had to deliver early. We were rejected from two high-risk hospitals due to being, well, too high-risk(?). But the reality was, we needed a facility that accommodated neonatal, cardiac, and obstetric specialists, with an ICU for Nicola and NICU for Edison.

I will forever remember when Edison was born. It was the

happiest I had ever been, followed instantly by the most helpless and scared I had ever felt. It wasn't the delivery that posed the risk; it was the drop in my wife's blood pressure that could cause her heart to fail. Edison went one way, and Nicola went the other. As a husband and a new dad, I needed to choose which hallway to walk down; there is no right or wrong choice here.

As the birth was right before Christmas, and both Nicola and Edison were in their respective ICUs, we managed to arrange for Nicola to visit Edison as midnight approached on 24th December so we could be together for Edison's first Christmas. Ultimately, we made it through these initial tough challenges.

Being a dad has made me simultaneously want to be both at work and be happy never to return to an office. I would gladly stay home with my son. In fact, I took parental leave for nearly three months as the primary carer, despite the awkward discussions with my then Detective Senior Sergeant who, like a caricature from yesteryear, did what he thought was the right thing to do by taking me aside and warning me how this was bad for my career. This didn't deter me from accessing my entitlement, and yes, we are lucky to be in this country (Australia) and have access to this type of leave, irrespective of gender. I took this leave because I wanted to – it was important for me to be there, both to support my wife, and to witness the wonder of this new life we had brought into the world.

During this time, my wife was away from work for nine months, partly due to needing open-heart surgery. Not to be dramatic, but it was a whirlwind first year into fatherhood when, at times, we confronted the possibility of me going it alone. Like in Mumbai, when confronted with literal life or death scenarios, your priorities are oddly clear. I engaged my Employee Assistance Program (EAP) and was able to talk to a professional. I'd like to reiterate how lucky we are in Australia to have these types of services as a standard in most workplaces.

Always eager to add more onto the pile of 'life', we became

pregnant again—almost six months to the day—after Nicola's surgery. During this time, Nicola had returned to work in Human Resources. Reflecting on the bureaucracy and dated thinking of my previous Detective Senior Sergeant, I again didn't hesitate to take three months of parental leave when Terrence arrived in 2020. As if to prove my point about how little this would impact my career, the following year I was promoted; two years later, I left my comfort zone, resigned from policing, and transitioned to a government position as an Assistant Director. That transition was relatively easy compared to the adjustment of having a second child. Having a second child is not twice the work, it is more work, but the challenge is in the lack of sleep, and less down time – the wisdom of "you nap when they nap" is crushed by a two-year-old who wants to show you how fast he can run, jump, or tip out the entire box of LEGO. This newfound baby joy comes fully stocked with needing to be in a constant state of readiness of choosing the least bad option – allowing the least harmful action whilst embracing the constant noise.

After Terrence was born, I decided to go back to university to study a Master of Leadership and Management remotely at night. This seemed like a good idea, but it was another thing to add to the 'life' pile. My wife was working fly-in fly-out at times on a 2:1 roster as a Human Resources Business Partner for a non-profit aged care provider (and was also studying a master's degree). Life was chaos. Yes, actual chaos. For a short time, I balanced front-line police duties (on a three-panel shift of days, afternoons, and nights) and sole parenting a two-year-old and a six-month-old before being promoted as a Prosecuting Sergeant. Policing is not an industry that is as flexible as some other roles. But a decade in policing taught me crisis management, and two out of three weeks, that was how we lived. Routine became our saviour, as Jocko Willink states, *discipline equals freedom.*

Waking up at 5:30am daily may seem like a push, but the alternate is worse. One morning, our adventurous two-year-old,

Edison, who was in a clubfoot brace, fearlessly tried to take on our staircase despite not being able to move his legs independently. But we were there to prevent any potential harm. Our early morning wake-ups allow for our sons to explore their limits with parental oversight, although their curiosity typically guides them to the fridge. Life consisted of breakfast, daycare drop-offs, praying no urgent calls came whilst I was in court, escaping work, squeezing in a trip to the park, realising I forgot to get dinner, eating cereal for dinner, bedtime routine, quick tidy and/or washing (choose your fight), then sitting back at the dining room table to read endless academic articles, and learning how to write post-grad university papers. Yes, that kind of chaos.

The trick was realising that you were always going to get through the day, and sometimes cereal is ok for dinner. It's about balance, not a restful Zen—we are talking parenting! It's about sitting down before bed, reflecting on the million tasks that were meant to happen, realising the important ones were done, the kids had clothes for the next day, there was milk in the fridge (we had litres and litres taking up a whole shelf—not a door sleeve, a shelf!), and the other tasks can wait. There was a solid three-month period when my lawn did its own thing – as far as priorities go, the front grass didn't make the cut... nailed it! Dad jokes are the real social currency.

As Nicola's career progressed from a HR Business Partner to the Australasian HR Manager of a global company, I looked for more ways to actively encourage and support her. Policing had, up to that point, dictated where we lived, reduced our family time (due to shift work and weekend duties), and, upon reflection, had been a disproportionate focus.

We were in the fortunate position of splitting the public/private industries, and it was clear that my entitlements were more generous, with two weeks of carer's leave, unlimited sick leave, and unshakable job security. I have always been the emergency contact, primary carer, the first port of call for kid-related matters. In a household where both parents work, I encourage you to plan out who is going to leave work to deal with mini-emergencies based on the entitlements available through your respective employers. If in doubt, befriend your HR liaison or read the policies—don't shy away from a discussion due to assumptions you make about what's normal at work. By not having open conversations or knowing the variables, you may make poor decisions that leave you financially worse off, stressed out, or potentially overloading your partner with competing demands.

The impacts of COVID were not felt by everyone in society equally. In our household, it barely changed our routine as policing was not a work-from-home affair, and being a first responder held our daycare place. Western Australia, for the most part of 2020/21, had an elimination strategy with zero community transmission. But the fear was real, the unknown consequences of how this would affect the kids' health long term if they contracted the virus scared me. The social isolation this fear caused limited the support we had with other family members who lived in WA. To add to this isolation, Nicola's mother and grandparents lived in the Eastern States and didn't see Terrence until he was two. This was similar to my brother who lived in the UK.

As I began making decisions about my future outside of policing, I decided to take my long service leave. With COVID restrictions easing, and being a glutton for punishment, we seized the opportunity to book a 17-hour flight to London. I knew this was one of the last chances to get Terrence on a free flight; at two years old, everyone gets a seat. Nicola had limited time off, and after a couple of weeks, she enjoyed a relaxing solo flight back to Perth. The boys and I stayed with my brother and his wife in London, exploring the museums, galleries, and every park between Uxbridge and London Bridge. It was an amazing, challenging, and at times, frustrating five weeks. I took thousands of photos, and recently reminisced about Terrence erupting in a fit of rage in the National Gallery as we stood next to Van Gogh's *Sunflowers*.

It wasn't long before I admitted defeat and we went to another park. I know it was an experience Edison will remember forever, something I will treasure. And the solo parent flight back? I stood for a good 12 hours to maximise the chances of the boys sleeping and am still recovering from seeing the Paw Patrol movie being looped 11 times in a row. Again, it's about getting through each day and counting the wins.

I returned from the London trip, transitioned careers, and encountered a whole new set of challenges at work. Yet, I established clear boundaries: after-school time is family time, sunshine equals park time, and weekends are reserved for fishing, camping, and adventures. I have found my balance by setting these boundaries, realising that one sleep-in past sunrise a week is enough, and focusing on one thing at a time is the best way forward.

My life cannot be replicated, and I would navigate it the same way if presented with the same information. Life's lessons are hard-fought; what works for me does so because of the experiences I have had. I sense the expectation of offering advice on achieving balance or pointing out the flawed logic in thinking my circumstance provides insight into how parenting should work. However, the reality is that parenting is highly subjective. The values, styles, and imperatives you hold dear and relentlessly try to impart onto your kids are yours. The only advice I can give with any passion is: be kind to yourself, don't measure your success by other people's circumstances, reach out for help (dads' groups exist because there is a need for them), lean on your entitlements, and use your EAPs.

As a dad, you get to shape reality for your kids, setting the example of how to act, what is worth your time, how to treat your peers, and what relationships look like. It may sound overwhelming, but like all of life's gifts, it's a series of adventures—there will be some hard bits, some funny bits, some sad, scary, joyous, and brilliant moments. Being a dad is by far my most dominant identity trait, and I am proud of it; you should be too.

ROLFE PIKE

> CHILDREN LEARN BY OBSERVING,
> DON'T UNDERESTIMATE HOW
> IMPORTANT THE FIRST SEVEN
> YEARS ARE IN CREATING A CHILD'S
> PARADIGMS AND THE WAY THEY
> VIEW THE WORLD.

Rolfe Pike is a hands-on dad with a mission for global domination while juggling home responsibilities. His unique blend of business acumen and parenting is driven by a passion for helping SME business owners, utilising his tech expertise and Global Engineering MBA. Outside work, he's a water enthusiast who enjoys fishing and water sports. Inspired by leaders like Richard Branson and Elon Musk, Rolfe's entrepreneurial spirit thrives on innovation and genuine connections. Through his adventures, he hopes to inspire fellow dads, highlighting the delicate balance of global ambitions and cherished family moments.

ROLFE PIKE

AUTHOR NAME: ROLFE PIKE
BUSINESS NAME: PAMWE GROUP
POSITION: FOUNDER
LINKEDIN: LINKEDIN.COM/IN/ROLFE-PIKE

I was very blessed growing up. I was an only child and grew up in Zimbabwe. My dad owned a group of businesses, and my mum was a stay-at-home mum who looked after me, with the help of a maid. I was an only child. I was subjected to a lot of my parents' adult friends, which made me comfortable and confident in communicating with older people. In no way did I have the fanciest 'things', but I was never short of anything either. I was raised to be humble and appreciative. My parents were both very supportive and loving, and I am extremely grateful for the upbringing I had.

My childhood was magical! We had a boathouse on a lake 45-minutes out of town, and I was encouraged to get out on the water as often as possible. Something I still try to do today. It was sociable and it created an incredible community around me. From the age of 10 I was allowed to drive the boat myself. I cherished the responsibility my parents gave me, and I seldom broke their trust. Some of my fondest memories were of a typical Sunday, when my parents would come out to the boathouse and cook up a roast pork feast for me and my friends. We would be on the water almost all day, pop back around lunchtime, eat like we had never seen food before, and then head back onto the water. I hope to provide an equivalent lifestyle for my children, something I am still working on.

My upbringing inspires me to provide my children with diverse experiences and valuable skillsets, aiming to nurture them into well-rounded individuals grounded in humility, respect, and responsibility.

When my daughter was born, my wife and I were living in Dubai at the time and paternity leave wasn't a thing. After a rough delivery, my wife was not herself for a few days, which meant I was Johnny-on-the-spot for responding to the little one! We were in hospital for about a week, my employers were none the wiser that I had even had a child! I worked off my laptop and juggled phone calls between feeding times and nappy changes in the hospital. At work, I became the ultimate 'dad-juggler'—no diapers, just deadlines!

When my son arrived, we had been living in Australia for around three years and I was working for a large organisation. My wife's parents came over for three months to help, so I thought I would save my paternity leave for when they had left. However, when I went to take it, my organisation told me I was no longer eligible, and I lost my ability to use it. To this day I still regret not having some time off when my children were born. These are precious moments you don't get back in life and I wish I could have the chance to do it again and take some time off.

My wife has been the primary caregiver while I focused on bringing in the money. Despite this, I have always tried to be as hands-on as possible. Running my own business provides me the flexibility to actively engage in my children's lives. This involves coaching my sons in under 7s rugby, accompanying my daughter to netball coaching and games during the week and weekends, and assisting with school runs when needed.

I grew up in an era where mothers looked after the kids and fathers earned the money. Typically, during that time, dads had very little to do with the 'duties' of raising kids other than being the final threat of a beating with a belt—or a similar weapon, like a 'Sjambok'! Dads did the 'fun' things, such as taking them hunting, shooting, fishing, riding motorbikes, or, in my case, driving cars and boats. I have so many good memories of going boating and riding motorbikes with my dad.

I have always been mindful of giving my wife a break when she needs one. She does a lot in the house and now works part-time. I think it is really important that she has some time to herself, and I encourage her to do so as much as we can.

My wife works part-time from home while also managing to run the house and take care of the kids. It's amazing what she manages to fit in her day! I have huge respect for what mums are able to achieve in a day! It's incredible what you can do when you can multitask! As we all know boys can't multitask, so please never ask me to (ha-ha!). I always supported my wife in going back to work as I felt it would give her a sense of contribution and freedom with earning her own money, I also felt she needed the adult interaction and other focuses rather than just the kids. I like to think that we have created a good balance where I can help out where I can, and it allows her to work and get the stimulation she needs. Admittedly, I initially found it challenging when my wife went back to work. I felt guilty for not helping enough or being proactive with jobs around the house, but it was (and still is) something I work on for myself and for her. It's hard to fit everything in, but we manage it as best as we can.

I believe I have a strong relationship with my children because I have built trust with them. Allowing myself the flexibility to be part of their interests enables me to be present with them and build those relationships.

It's tricky as they grow up and the dynamics start to change, especially when trying to navigate the differences between boys and girls. They both have different wants and needs, so my wife and I work out the best way to adapt to each of their personal needs as best as we can. We always praise our children when they do well and maintain firm boundaries. We have always taken an approach of being firm but fair. Although I probably won't let my son take out a boat on his own at 10 years old, I acknowledge the world has changed a lot, and we do not have the liberties and freedoms I had growing up. That being said, I will always encourage their independent spirit and hope to be part of both of their adventures.

Just like anything in life, it's important to have a break to allow you to reset. This goes for raising kids too. When we had our second child, we had only recently moved to Australia, we didn't really know anyone, we were continents away from both of our families, and our friends were over 45-minutes away! If I was to have my time again, I would I ensure we had a support network nearby in those early years, either grandparents or friends that we could have as part of our lives. It would have made such a difference for our family, especially for my wife. I have no doubt it would have been better for the kids and grandparents as well!

Small kids just want your attention – work and social media can come later! Appreciate their attention while they want yours! In no time at all, they become tweens, then teenagers, and we all know what teenagers are like!

If I were to give advice to other dads, I would say:

Be present. Actively engage with them. Don't let the TV or your smartphone take your attention away from just being with them.

Take leave. If you can afford to take time off when your children are born, do it. Spend time with them from the beginning—you'll never get that time back.

It often feels like one can never do enough. Children learn by observing, don't underestimate how important the first seven years are in creating a child's paradigms and the way they view the world. This can either set them up to fly sky-high or struggle endlessly! Time spent together in the early years will form a bond that is forever unbreakable.

Set a positive example; your children are watching you at all times! Whether you are aware of it or not. Stop and think: Are you demonstrating the values and behaviours you wish to instil in them through your own actions?

Show respect, kindness, and patience, even in challenging situations. I rate communication as one of the most important interpersonal skillsets. Every evening we have dinner together, this gives everyone a platform to speak about their day and talk through any challenges, observations, or successes they might have had. Parenting isn't about *not* doing anything wrong, it's about providing a safe space to communicate with your family about their wants and needs, and yours too.

ROWYN BARTLETT

TIME INVESTED INTENTIONALLY
TODAY WILL REAP A HARVEST IN
YEARS TO COME—IT'S NEVER
WASTED!

Rowyn is a husband, father, and leader—a people-focused individual determined to find balance in life so that the lives around him can flourish. He is dedicated to being a role model for his kids by challenging himself through ultra-running, demonstrating that we can overcome challenges in life.

ROWYN BARTLETT

AUTHOR NAME: ROWYN BARTLETT
BUSINESS NAME: WESTERN POWER
POSITION: CONTRACT MANAGER
BUSINESS INDUSTRY: UTILITIES
LINKEDIN: LINKEDIN.COM/IN/ROWYN-BARTLETT-56B45A49

My parents moved around a bit in the early years and eventually came to settle in a small country town called Ixopo, which is located in Kwa-Zulu Natal, South Africa. Some of the best childhood memories were in this town. I can remember all my friends would live just a few streets apart and we would often all meet up after lunch or dinner on the weekends and in school holidays and we would play all sorts of games. We'd build forts and make up all sorts of fun games that would keep us out of the house for hours, often until we'd have our parents calling out for us to come home. My family was quite close back then. My uncles, aunties, and grandparents all lived in close proximity to each other, so I really got to experience the positive impact of being raised not only by my parents but my broader family too. It's like the saying goes, "It takes a village." Some of my young uncles were into off-road racing, fast cars, and motorbikes. They were mechanics by trade which meant they were always working on some sort of vehicle, probably one that went really fast. I'd have the opportunity to go to their workshop and either see them working on trucks and cars or watch them race their off-road buggies. There were other times I would go into the hardware store that my granddad ran, or I'd head to the bank after school where my mum would work. My dad even ran a general store that I sometimes went to after school.

Work was always a normal part of life, and my parents always did their best to look after us while balancing the needs of running a household and providing for their family. We were not the most well-off family, and from recent conversations with my mum, there were some really tough times in the early years when my sister and I were young. My parents knew they had to work hard to provide and look after us, so both my parents worked full-time. However, I never had this feeling of, "I wish my parents didn't work so much." My sister and I just got accustomed to how things were; this is what you do—you work, you provide for your family, and sometimes the kids come along for the ride.

Looking back now, I realise how lucky I was—especially with the weight parents carry by wanting to provide the best for their children. My parents showed us that you can work and provide for your family; you just have to be intentional about keeping things balanced. They never saw kids as an inconvenience or a reason why you can't do or be a part of certain things. They just put us in the mix of things, and yes, there probably were times we would have been bored out of our minds or didn't want to be somewhere, but we had to be because it was important for the bigger picture.

If I had to sum up my childhood in one word, the word 'adventure' comes to mind. Life was full of adventures. Not because of extravagant holidays or fancy materialistic things but because of the simplicity of the adventures we'd create in the back garden, the mountain trails, the walks to the dam to fish, or the bike rides through the plantations. My parents probably never realised it at the time, but they gave us the best adventures by allowing us the freedom to explore and create our own fun, it also meant we were out the house so it worked for them at times too (ha-ha)!

This goes to show that when we intentionally work towards

leading a more balanced life, we can provide a life full of adventure for our children. The greatest memory I have as a child is every July, for three or four years, my parents, family, friends, and extended family would all go away to a coastal town for two weeks. It was nothing fancy, but they made the best memories. The two weeks were full of fishing, roasting marshmallows, making friends, playing cricket, joking, laughing, and just spending time together.

The greatest gift my parents worked to give us was time, mostly being simplistic moments where we could just connect. And the greatest gift we can give our own kids is time; it's something they will crave more than anything else. I recently took my kids to the leisure centre for a swim in the pool, and my daughter turned to me and said, "You're the best dad!" She wanted time with me, and I gave her that undivided time, even if we were doing something simple like going for a swim.

In the blink of an eye, everything can change. The time you thought you had can be taken just like that, with absolutely no option to rewind the clock. I experienced this when I lost my dad to cancer when I was 12. I went away to a friend's house, and a few days later, I arrived home to a life without my father. Words could never describe how I felt and still feel to this day. Knowing that I will never get that time back with my dad was by far one of the most painful experiences I have ever had to endure. My heart ached just to see him one more time. What I would give even now to just chuck the rods in the back of the ute and wet a line with him.

I have only recently come to see the impact that living a more balanced life can have on my family and myself. About a year ago, I made the decision to quit a job I had been at for little over 13 years. It was a job that was literally demanding more and more of my time, even to the point where it would be the last thing I'd be thinking about at night and the first thing in the morning. Work began to consume me and my time, slowly eroding my ability to be a present husband, father, and friend. Would I even be able to find a place to work where I will be challenged and stimulated and that would not consume me entirely to the point that I wouldn't be present with my children and my wife?

Ever since our son was born in 2015, all my wife wanted was to be a present mum. Her current work structure is three shifts a fortnight, an arrangement we have been able to make work since having our two kids and something we are making work to this day. We both know the positive impact this arrangement has on our kids, especially in these early years.

We have often tossed up the idea of buying a bigger house, but this would more than likely mean I would have to take a higher paying job that has the potential to take more of my time, or my wife would need to work more, which would take time away from where it's needed most. We've settled on keeping the smaller house but a lower mortgage because we've agreed that the trade-off just isn't worth it for us and what we want for our family.

This is how we currently share the load between us: when my wife works in the afternoon, the kids go to a friend's house after school, then I pick them up when I finish work and take them home. I then take care of homework, dinner, prep the lunches for the next day, and handle the general night-time routine. Although I could still improve at washing the dishes, or so my wife would probably say (ha-ha!). On other days, we usually work together to share the evening routine. On the weekends when my wife has to work, I look after the kids. We usually end up at the pools, visiting the grandparents, or having a Nintendo or movie night – and I'm sure there is some ice cream involved somewhere!

Over eight months ago I found a workplace that offered me everything I needed and more. I currently work as a Contract Manager in the utility industry. I am challenged professionally, get to contribute to meaningful work, and provide a service to the community. I'm able to be a part of an amazing team of people who make work fun, who challenge me to be better, and encourage a work-life balance. The positive impact this job has had on me and my family is priceless! It has allowed me the space to grow as a professional but also as a husband and father.

I think the biggest challenge with the balance we have created as a family is trying not to get caught up in the comparison trap. In this day and age, we are flooded with everyone's 'perfect' social media lifestyle – the big house, fancy cars, extravagant holidays, and all this materialistic stuff that sometimes makes you feel as though this is what your family needs. In reality, none of it is ever what they need. A lot of 'stuff' can create imbalance, and it's something my wife and I are not willing to trade-off for our family. We are happy to settle for what others may see as less because we know that we are actually gaining more. This doesn't mean that those who can provide all that 'stuff' are living an imbalanced life, but sometimes the 'stuff' substitutes the time. And, in my opinion, it's not worth it.

As I reflect back on my journey as a father, the advice I would give is not to get caught up in the trap of thinking it's 'stuff' your kids need. Ultimately, it's you they want. Yes, by all means spoil the kids when you can and give them the best you can afford, but remember, all they want is time with you. Look for opportunities to invest time in them. This could be taking a half-day off work to pick them up from school, taking time out to go to the pools, camping in the backyard, playing cars or dolls, or even just watching one of their favourite movies together. Time invested intentionally today will reap a harvest in years to come—it's never wasted!

As dads, it is critical to live a balanced life, not just for our own mental and physical health but for the development of our children and the strengthening of our relationships. Remember, the balancing act is just that—an act. It is something we will intentionally work on for the rest of our lives. When we intentionally make an effort to find that balance, the lives of those closest to us are positively impacted. The greatest gift you can give is time, and there are many things fighting to take that from you. Be sure to invest your time wisely.

BARRY MONE

" YOU KNOW THAT THERE'S GOING TO BE AN END POINT FOR CHARLIE, BUT IF YOU WANT TO LOOK AT IT IN ANY KIND OF POSITIVE WAY, EVERYONE HAS AN END POINT. WE ARE FORTUNATE, IN A WAY, TO APPRECIATE THE TIME WE HAVE WITH HIM AS WE KNOW IT WILL BE SOONER THAN OTHERS. "

Barry is a Resources Travel Manager, with a background in both Corporate and WA Mining Travel, and father to both Charlie 14 and Khloe 13, Happy married to Kristy, we have a beautiful family, Born in Scotland, I grew up in South West London, where I met Kristy, Kristy returned to Perth, and I emigrated to WA in Early 2005 we married in 2007, with Charlie arriving in 2009 and Khloe in 2011, Perth is now home for us all

BARRY MONE

NAME: BARRY MONE
ROLE: ADVOCATE AND CARER.
COMPANY: CHARLIES HOPE
LINKEDIN: WWW.LINKEDIN.COM/IN/BARRY-MONE-B500B320/

SARAH:
Can you tell me about your childhood and how you were raised?

BARRY:
Okay, so I was born in Scotland and moved to London when I was seven. Dad couldn't get into the Scottish prison service, but it was easy to get into the English prison service.

He was a prison guard and stayed in that job for close to 30 years. Being a Scottish person growing up in London was quite challenging, but I had my brother and sister around. We lived in a normal three-bedroom house.

SARAH:
Was your mum around? And did she work or stay at home?

BARRY:
Mum went back to work after my brother and I started school. And living where we lived was great! It was very accessible to London, surrounding southwest of London, and we lived quite a stable family life. We went on family holidays. It was a pretty

normal upbringing. And when I was 16, I got a job in the travel industry.

SARAH:
When did you move to Perth?

BARRY:
So, I came to Perth in 2005.

SARAH:
Did you move with your wife or did you meet her here?

BARRY:
My wife Kristy is Australian. She's from Perth. She had a visa in the UK. And we met in the July 2003. Kristy worked for Flight Centre, massive company here. My company got invited to their London award ceremony event and the rest is history. But as the story goes, Kristy was coming to the end of her four-year Ancestry Visa and while it wasn't the case of if she wanted to come home or needed to come home – it was just her time. And so she said to me, "I'm going home. Are you coming?" Back in 2000 I was offered a free trip after the Sydney Olympics and said, "No Thanks – too far," but low and behold, now I'm here in Perth.

SARAH:
How great! Tell me about your children.

BARRY:
Okay, so I've got two children. Charlie is currently 14 and his younger sister, Khloe, is 12.

SARAH:
Can you tell me about Charlie's special needs?

BARRY:

Charlie is fully disabled. He's now currently non-ambulant. His condition is Duchenne muscular dystrophy, which we call DMD for short. It's a degenerative muscle condition. We've had people quite recently who thought it just affected his legs, but to put it into perspective, it affects every muscle in his body. Before he was officially diagnosed, he had some choking issues.

SARAH:

Tell me about Charlie's childhood and when you found out that he had muscular dystrophy?

BARRY:

Okay, so Charlie was diagnosed at eight years old in November 2017.

SARAH:

Which is late, right?

BARRY:

Very, very late. The average diagnosis is between 18-months and three or four. Charlie was very okay with his milestones, but he also had a condition called PHPV—persistent hyperplastic primary vitreous meaning he is technically blind in one eye. He had a cataract removed from his left eye and has an Intraocular lens to help with vision to magnify the vision because the sunlight doesn't penetrate behind his eye.

One cataract is from his PHPV with taking steroids because of his Duchenne condition, and he actually formed a second cataract in his other eye. You can only ever have one cataract in each eye. Cataracts are primarily for older people. Charlie had one removed and then he got one in the other eye. They say it will be a standard removal – but I'll believe it when I see it. Well, that's what we were told originally – we were told standard. It wasn't until the doctor

BARRY MONE

169

investigated that he found out what the condition was. That was when he about age two, and it affected his peripheral vision and his balance. So, everything that we didn't spot was DMD was because of that.

The choking was one thing, because people don't understand the muscles in the throat – the tongue, the jaw, everything. The doctor suggested it was reflux, beggar's belief. But that's an obvious solution to a not so simple situation. It wasn't until he started falling over that we realised we've got an issue here. But when you tell your son to stop walking on his tiptoes—that's an obvious sign. Or when you tell your son to lift his feet—that's also an obvious sign. I would say to him, "Charlie, if you lift your feet, you won't trip over." Well, we thought he was tripping over but it was obviously a lot more than that. His muscles were failing, and that made me feel so bad as a parent.

Charlie had an instance quite recently in his wheelchair where he cracked a bone on his foot. I mean, how a boy who sits down can break his foot is laughable! He's had a couple of instances where he hasn't switched off his wheelchair, and he was taking off his jumper and, somehow, he moved his wheelchair forward and squashed his foot. We had just had a four-hour appointment with a neurologist on the Friday, and by the Sunday, which was Father's Day, this happened, and we went straight back to hospital. The doctors said it was fine at the time, but it turned out to be a fracture in his foot. And the joke I made about it at the hospital was that of course he will take it easy because he sits down in the wheelchair—it's not like he's going to put pressure on it!

SARAH:
Yeah – so he deteriorated as time went on? You got the diagnosis around the age of eight. What have you had to put into place as a parent for yourself and your wife to manage dealing with a child that is in a wheelchair essentially?

BARRY:

So, Charlie was in primary school, and we had to go through the whole disability setup at the school with ramps, and he had his mobility scooter at the time, so we had to make sure that was accessible to and from school for him. Ramps, guardrails, things like that at school. At home we've got ramps at the front door, back door, and side door, we've had rails put on the toilet, now we've had the whole bathroom developed into a modified bathroom. The next stage will be a setup for Charlie's hospital bed, for lack of a better word. It's a mechanical aid that can do everything. There are obviously no rails on the side yet, which he may need down the line. We've got a manual hoist that we don't use as Charlie's not comfortable with the manual hoist – it takes quite a lot to strap it around him to make him secure. Then you lift him up and lift him down. So, we're looking at ceiling hoists now which are a big modification. That will be for his bedroom and potentially the bathroom as well. You're looking at up to $25,000 in funding to do that. In terms of modifications in his room, his lights are automatic, his blinds are automatic, his fan is automatic – it's all voice controlled.

SARAH:

And how have you and your wife had to adapt your lives for Charlie? Did your wife go back to work after having Charlie?

BARRY:

Yes, she did. So Kristy has worked from home since the pandemic. She's now currently, for lack of a better word, a full-time carer. There might be the need for her to go back to work at some point, but it's finding that sort of great job with the right balance.

SARAH:

Yes. And that's been the case for yourself as well, right? Making sure that you've got the balance?

BARRY:

Yeah, still working full-time, but having the balance and flexibility to do what you need to do to support Charlie is very important. And that can be anything from making sure you can get to school ok in winter when it's raining, or even in summer, we can't just say get on the bus on a 40-degrees day. He's unable to regulate his body temperature, so it's not as simple as popping up an umbrella on a sunny day to keep the heat off you, Charlie needs a lot more than that. We've got to weather check every day from winter through to summer.

SARAH:

And how have you found the response from employers? Have you had any issues with your need for flexibility or has it always been fairly well received?

BARRY:

It's been well received to an extent, but I've also had challenges, definitely. But it's about finding that balance. I've been through the challenges of having to tell my employer when he was diagnosed, and then going into new employment and navigating how open to be in the interview.

SARAH:

How do you manage that? Do you tell employers upfront or do you wait until you've started before you have that discussion?

BARRY:

It comes with the territory of me doing a lot of social media to raise awareness. The story is well known locally so the previous, probably, five employers were already aware of it.

SARAH:

That's good. And have you found any real challenges in terms of how to make that balance or have you figured it out as best as you can?

BARRY:

My biggest challenge is in our current world; everybody would love to work from home. There's a need, a must, and a want. My want is not to have to work from home five days a week—it's not just a want, but a need. It's important to get your happiness as well, right? It's got to be a balance with that as well. That's what I forget.

SARAH:

You are just as important.

BARRY:

That's my biggest take away of hearing someone talk about a challenge in their life and their mental health. My focus has always been so much on Charlie. If you did a check on my mental health and my physical health at the moment, who knows? I probably shouldn't say that...

SARAH:

No, but it's true. And that's one of the things that we've found throughout the whole book, to be honest, is the importance to bring it back to yourself because you being the best version of yourself is the best thing for your kids, your wife, and everything else.

BARRY:

If I'm not around, if I break a bone, we're back to square one. And it's not just me, it's the whole family. The whole support system. If any of that breaks down, we're back to square one.

SARAH:

So how do you keep it going?

BARRY:
You just have to.

SARAH:
Do you and your wife do anything to keep your relationship together? And I mean, it's so challenging what you've had to go through, how have you dealt with it as a couple?

BARRY:
We deal with it more as a family. My daughter's just about to get genetically tested. We've gotten to the point when we're going to, say the neurologist, Charlie's understanding enough now, and we say to him, "If you've got any questions for the doctors then you can ask too." He's taking an active interest as well at the moment, and so we give the same respect to his sister when she attends appointments. Her biggest thing, at the moment, is getting genetically tested.

SARAH:
Is she getting genetically tested to see if she carries the gene?

BARRY:
So, Kristy is the carrier, right? So it's a 50/50 chance that she would be a carrier. We know the mother is the carrier.

SARAH:
Yes. Right. Is it anywhere else in the family?

BARRY:
No, there's no one else in the family. My wife's the carrier and that's why my daughter has to get genetically tested to see if she is a carrier too. Because if she had children... that's the biggest crux.

SARAH:

And how are you going to manage that? If she's told that she's a carrier at the age of 12/13, that's such a heavy load for her?

BARRY:

Well, it gives her time to adjust, to manage expectations and I guess make decisions. I mean there's so many things around it now, you can clean genetics. By the time she's 17 or 18, she may have a boyfriend and then she's got to think twice. She will be clearing her mind as to what she has to do. Whereas the suggestion is getting it checked at 16 or 18, so she has no time to prepare and make the right decision. And if she wants it, then it's nice to be able to give her that option to do it, we think. It's important for her. And I think we've got to that stage now. Whereas with her, she wants to know what the outcome is, deal and manage that. But is it a yes? Is it no?

SARAH:

Yeah. And she would've had to have been quite mature in her upbringing due to dealing with Charlie, throughout her life anyway, so she's very exposed to that situation, and it makes sense why she would want to know.

BARRY:

Charlie is very aware of his course of life and what he is to expect. But what we also have to prepare for in the background is that she will become an only sibling at some point. The life expectancy of someone with DMD is 26 and Charlie is currently 14.

We had a conversation like that on the weekend. We were at the 'Save our Sons' family lunch in Perth at the SOS Foundation where we met a new family. Their son was about 18 months old. We were talking, and I said to the mother, "Have you got any more kids? Are you planning?" It's natural to ask questions like that, but they've got all these other implications involved as to whether having another child will lead to the same problems. It's stressful. And that's the crux of it. They are going to lose their one and only child. We don't know how we would handle that situation.

SARAH:
And you're lucky in a way that you have another child that is healthy, right?

BARRY:
We hope so. Well, it doesn't make it any easier, but knowing that will come one day, it's hard. I wouldn't want for my daughter to become the only sibling, but I also wouldn't want to be in the position of losing my only child.

SARAH:
I think it's a lose-lose situation.

BARRY:
We know families that may lose multiple children because they've got multiple children with it in their family. We know a family with three children, including twins, and the two boys have it—the eldest and one of the twins—so their daughter will lose both her brothers.

SARAH:
How do you deal with your own mental health in terms of preparing yourself for this situation?

BARRY:
To be honest, I dive in headfirst. It's the only way I know how. It's the only thing that I feel I'm capable of doing.

SARAH:
To cope?

BARRY:

To cope. Yeah. I can't have the regret of looking back and thinking I didn't do anything. There'll always be the question of, "Could I have done it better?"

SARAH:

I think you've done a pretty good job. But you know what the outcome is going to be. So, I guess it's preparing yourself as a family too?

BARRY:

Yes, we try to be prepared, but it's not easy. We do what we can to raise awareness, but we are not a charity unfortunately which has been a huge challenge.

SARAH:

No, you're about raising awareness.

BARRY:

The one benefactor thing on a charity is the biggest obstacle we face. Now my thoughts on a foundation would be down the line, but as I said previously, does this all stop when Charlie passes away? I don't think it does.

SARAH:

I don't think it does.

BARRY:

I think the biggest obstacle we faced was raising awareness and looking at the past, whether it be the fundraising for the accessible vehicle or organising the very first fundraiser event, people always associate it with just raising funds. So, while it has always been critical for the vehicle to give Charlie better quality of life, we—as a family—can only contribute so much to the quality of life and life experiences he deserves. We will always provide for Charlie, but we're not in a position to provide him with the experiences we feel he deserves. So, challenges lie in facilitating those kind of activities, like getting him on a plane, or anything we do to create memories or experiences for Charlie and the family.

SARAH:
Have you gotten him on a plane?

BARRY:
Not since our last big trip in May 2018. He was starting to struggle to walk, but he could still walk. And that's the principle again, in my perception, I can't stage photos, people might see photos of him standing from way back and they won't realise that he physically can't sit himself up in bed anymore.

SARAH:
If you were to give advice to another family that was going through a similar thing, what would you say?

BARRY:
We were always told that hope is the only thing we've got left. Just enjoy the time with the kids because believe it or not, you won't get that time back.

SARAH:
And I think that goes whether your child has a disability or not, right? It's appreciation of your time because you just don't know.

BARRY:
I think, and I'm not pointing the finger at parents that are not in my situation, but I think it's more important. Because well, you know that there's going to be an end point for Charlie, but if you want to look at it in any kind of positive way, everyone has

an end point. We are fortunate, in a way, to appreciate the time we have with him as we know it will be sooner than others. The irony with Charlie is, as he said to us, everyone has to go through something. That's why he hates it when things go wrong and that's when he gets upset with himself and says all the horrible things. But he accepts where he's at.

SARAH:
It's hard. Well, I think you have done an amazing job, for the record, and you continue to do amazing things to spread awareness, not just for Charlie, but for anyone that is going through or has been through something similar, so thank you.

SAM HILL

"

PARENTHOOD IS AN EVER-
EVOLVING JOURNEY, MARKED BY
THOSE MOMENTS THAT LEAVE AN
INDELIBLE MARK ON YOUR HEART.

"

Sam Hill, General Manager for Northern QLD at Coffey Testing, is a devoted father and advocate for work-life balance. With a background in geotechnics, sales, and leadership, Sam's career spans over nine years at Coffey Testing. He excels in building teams, particularly in a diverse geographic region, balancing a demanding career while actively participating in community initiatives. Sam is recognised for facilitating and hosting local events as a Community Facilitator for "Man With A Pram" and leading the "Dads Group" in partnership with Rockhampton Hospital. He is a certified Mental Health First Aider and has achieved an advanced diploma in laboratory operations. Sam's journey reflects his commitment to finding the ideal equilibrium between professional growth and family life.

SAM HILL

AUTHOR NAME: SAM HILL
BUSINESS NAME: COFFEY TESTING
POSITION: GENERAL MANAGER
BUSINESS INDUSTRY: CIVIL / GEOTECHNICAL
SOCIAL MEDIA: FACEBOOK.COM/SAM.HILL.9041083
LINKEDIN: LINKEDIN.COM/IN/SAMDAVIDHILL

Growing up as the oldest of six siblings, my childhood was marked by the unique dynamics of divorced parents. My mum, Karen, and dad, Dean, separated when I was just a toddler. They each remarried, introducing me to a blended family that would shape my perspective on work, family, and life.

Dad, with his unwavering work ethic, often had to juggle his professional commitments during our visits. Weekends were our special time together, and he made the most of those moments. Camping, fishing, 4-wheel driving, and boating adventures filled those precious hours. Looking back, I realise that my dad imparted more than just outdoor skills. He taught me the value of hard work and the idea that dedication pays off in the long run. Whether it was tightening the bolts on our 4WD before hitting Bribie Beach or instilling the importance of thorough preparation, he shaped my approach to work and success.

Although, I have often wondered: had my father taken more time off work during our visits, would I have embraced his strong work ethic and an unrelenting ambition to ascend the professional ranks, thereby setting the stage for the flexibility and freedom my current role provides me and my family?

On the other hand, my mum equipped me with invaluable life skills. From transforming last night's roast chicken into tonight's honey mustard masterpiece to the power of a tight-knit group of friends to weather life's storms, she instilled practical wisdom that I use daily. Her lessons are the foundation of my ability to thrive in the chaos of parenthood.

Today, I'm a husband to Emily and a father to three incredible kids: Parker, who's eight, Hudson, who is three, and our stillborn daughter, Aleisha, whom we lost in 2017. The ongoing pain and grief from losing Aleisha continues to be one of the most challenging parts of my life. Yet, we've found solace and purpose in actively participating in charitable endeavours, seeking to create a positive impact that honours her memory and legacy.

When it came to paternity leave, I made the most of the options available to me. With each of our three children, I took between two to four weeks off to be there during those crucial early moments of their lives. I would have loved to take more time off if circumstances allowed.

The reality is that someone in the family had to keep the financial wheels turning, and I was willing to make that sacrifice. This meant my wife could have the opportunity to stay home longer with our children, and it's a decision I've never regretted. It's a choice that many working dads like me face – juggling career responsibilities with the desire to be there for our children in those formative weeks.

During my first paternity leave with our oldest, Parker, my mother lived nearby. Her support and assistance was invaluable. However, it wasn't until the arrival of Hudson and my mother's move to Tasmania that I realised just how much of a help she had been. It's a stark reminder of the support network we sometimes take for granted and the adjustments we make when it's no longer readily available.

While I write down these thoughts I hold the role of General Manager for Northern QLD at Coffey Testing, a geotechnical and construction materials testing business. My professional journey is one that frequently takes me all over the state, with occasional trips to our other head offices sprinkled throughout the year. The role is a diverse one, often feeling like an insatiable bucket, ready to consume every drop of my attention. But the beauty of it is that I'm the one who controls the flow.

Flexibility is the lifeblood of my work. Averaging 10-hour days, I can pick and choose when and where those hours are spent. This flexibility has been a godsend, allowing me to be there for moments like the school run when I'm home and to complete my work after the kids are in bed. I'm profoundly grateful for this aspect of my work, which enables me to strike a balance between being a dedicated parent and a committed professional.

However, none of this would be possible without the unwavering support of my wife. We are a team in the truest sense, each playing a vital role in maintaining the delicate equilibrium between career and parenthood. Emily's watchful eye ensures that I don't tip the scales too far in one direction, providing an anchor that keeps me on course.

In the ever-evolving dance of work and parenting, flexibility and teamwork have become my trusted partners, allowing me to take on the role of a dedicated working dad with enthusiasm and determination.

When it came to Emily's return to work after each birth, it marked a significant juncture for our family. Approximately six months postpartum after Parker, Emily embarked on her journey back to the professional world. The transition, however, wasn't without its emotional weight.

As she took on the role of office manager at a law firm, there was an undeniable tinge of guilt that came with leaving Parker to go back to work. It's a sentiment that many working parents can relate to. But with a supportive network, especially my mother and a reliable daycare, we quickly found our rhythm.

Emily's professional path took an exciting turn when she pursued her teaching degree, leading to a position as a kindergarten teacher at a daycare centre. The natural synergy of having our second son, Hudson, attend that same daycare made the transition far smoother. Emily could regularly check in on him, offering reassurance and a deep connection during her working hours.

Just like other working parents, the return to work always brought changes to our household. The balance of home chores needed to adjust to Emily's working hours, and mornings and evenings sometimes became a mad rush as we juggled the demands of two careers and the needs of our growing family.

This chapter highlights the intricate dance of maintaining careers and nurturing a family, with both partners striving to find the right balance. It's a journey that comes with its share of challenges, but also moments of great growth and connection as we adapt to the evolving chapters of our lives.

Parenthood is an ever-evolving journey, marked by those moments that leave an indelible mark on your heart. For me, one such moment came when Parker took an interest in chess during a family holiday. It was one of those vacations where the usual board games like Connect 4 and Uno were conspicuously absent. In that void, Parker's competitive nature and strategic mind found a new passion in chess. I became his chess teacher, and soon, we were playing games most nights. As he improved, I even had to download an app to keep up with him! It's in these moments that I'm reminded of the wonderful complexities of parenthood—nurturing a child's interests, sharing their triumphs, and supporting their growth.

But there's more to these cherished moments than chess matches. It's the everyday joys that truly make this journey special. The thrill of coming home to the excited screams of "Daddy's home!" is a reminder that, even when work takes me away, the love of my children remains unwavering. It's witnessing their developmental milestones, from the first tentative crawl to those precious first words. It's giving them the courage to leap off that big rock into the creek and see them overcome their fears. I am incredibly grateful for the time I spend with my children – they become a source of motivation to create more of these cherished memories.

It's in the quiet moments, too, when I see my wife display her nurturing and caring nature. The softness she shows our children, the way she helps them grow emotionally, and the love she bestows upon them is a reminder that parenting is a shared journey.

As a father to young children, my relationship with them is an ongoing journey filled with learning, growth, and shared experiences. Parker, at the age of eight, is at a stage where he's beginning to explore his emotional depth. It's a beautiful phase to witness as he starts to forge his unique path in the world. I'm proud of the little person he's becoming, and the emotional growth is a reminder that our children are individuals with their own thoughts, feelings, and dreams.

Hudson, on the other hand, at just three years old, is in the stage where he wants to be my shadow. Much like his older brother did in his early years, Hudson is eager to mimic and participate in the activities I do. It's a joyful and endearing phase. As I see the world through his curious eyes, I am reminded of the influence parents have on their children.

My relationship with both of them is built on a foundation of love, shared experiences, and the unbreakable bond that parenthood brings. These early years are precious, and I look forward to the journey ahead as we continue to grow and learn together.

The journey of parenthood is marked by numerous decisions, moments, and choices, each with its own set of consequences. When asked if I would do anything differently in terms of balancing work and parenting, it's a question that stirs deep contemplation.

As a father who has experienced the heart-wrenching loss of a stillborn child, I am acutely aware of the profound impact that life's experiences can have. In the face of such a tragedy, it's only natural to wish for a different outcome, to give anything to change the past. But, in the words of a favourite song, "Every pebble in the water has a ripple effect, and every action will bear a consequence."

It's through the ups and downs, the stumbles, and the imperfections that my wife and I have learned some of life's most poignant lessons. We've grown as parents and as individuals, and these experiences have shaped our values and our approach to raising our children. Our imperfections are the source of valuable insights and the lessons we can, in turn, impart to our children when they become parents themselves.

Above everything, I'm proud of the parents we have become, with all our unique challenges and triumphs. If I were to do it all over again, I'd recognise that each experience, even the most painful, has a purpose in the intricate tapestry of parenthood.

Balancing the responsibilities of work and parenting is a dynamic journey, and it's a path where nothing is set in stone. As fathers, we must be willing to adapt and change with the ever-shifting landscape of our children's needs and our professional responsibilities. The key is to recognise that the balance is constantly evolving, just as our children are growing and changing.

Children can be resistant to change, but don't be afraid to try something different or new. Seek advice and insights from others who have walked this path before you. What works for one family may not work for another, so it's essential to gather a variety of perspectives and learn from both successes and challenges.

Above all, be kind to yourself. As parents, it's all too easy to fall into the trap of feeling like we're not doing enough. But know this: if you are trying and showing up for your children, you're already winning. Parenthood is a journey filled with ups and downs, and sometimes, all you need to do is keep trying, keep showing up, and keep giving your best.

In the end, the balance of work and parenting is a dance, and as fathers, we're learning the steps along the way. The most important thing is to keep moving, keep adapting, and, most importantly, keep cherishing the precious moments with your children.

STAN ROLFE

DOING WHAT MAKES YOU HAPPY
WILL ALLOW YOU TO SHOW UP
HAPPIER AND BE BETTER FOR YOUR
FAMILY.

Stan Rolfe describes himself as an average father with two awesome young boys, juggling life, work, and relationships, and striving to do better every day. He believes that finding the balance in everything you do, while prioritising yourself and surrounding yourself with good people, will help you achieve a richer, more prosperous life.

STAN ROLFE

AUTHOR NAME: STAN ROLFE
BUSINESS NAME: KEYWORDS STUDIOS AUSTRALIA
POSITION: HEAD OF TALENT ACQUISITION – APAC, CREATE SERVICE LINE
BUSINESS INDUSTRY: VIDEO GAMES
INSTAGRAM: @STANROLFE
X (TWITTER): @STANROLFE
LINKEDIN: LINKEDIN.COM/IN/STANROLFE

I was born on a small tropical island called Penang in Malaysia to an Australian father and a Malaysian mother. I am the eldest of four siblings, with two sisters and a brother. We spent our first years living in Penang where Dad was based for work as a mechanic for offshore oil rigs.

As a young boy growing up, Dad was often absent due to his rather protracted fly-in fly-out (FIFO) roster, which sometimes stretched anywhere between four to eight weeks away with only one or two weeks at home. Fortunately for Mum, she had support from a nanny. We moved to Perth, Western Australia, around the same time as Run DMC started hitting the charts in the mid-80s.

Growing up, I was much closer to my mother than my father. While we continued to have support from a nanny for a period of time, we all had to pitch in while Dad was away. Mum wasn't just a mum, but she also stepped into the role of being a dad too. She started working when Dad eventually left the oil game to start his own business. They both worked multiple jobs to keep up with bills and support four kids attending private school in the late-80s and early-90s, which eerily mirrors the economic times of today.

Dad was a great footy player, having played for Williams Narrogin with Barry Cable, a highly awarded Australian rules football player. I have a few memories of kicking the footy with Dad, but one of the most vivid memories I have was when he missed a particular footy game I wanted him to attend. This moment, along with my dad's absence and his passing seven years ago, has certainly laid the foundations for my approach to parenting. Dad and I had what I would describe as a distant relationship. I don't recall too many hugs or "Well done, son," type comments. I heard these indirectly through his brothers or friends. As I grew older and started thinking about being a parent, I swore to myself never to be absent from my kids, to show and tell them I loved them.

Today, I am a single parent with two sports-loving, life-loving boys aged 14 and 11 by the time this goes to print. Like most people, I envisaged living the normal family life in a normal family home; you know, Mum, Dad, kids, and a pet dog. That was the plan, Stan! Turns out, it did not go to plan.

At the time of my marital separation, the boys were about five and two. I had just come out of the hospital where my appendix was removed and found out I was being made redundant. This was a really challenging period – I had to start everything from scratch. I ended up moving into my sister's house, about a 40-minute drive from kids' mum's house and their schools. For those who are living in or know Perth's suburbs, the commute was from south of the river near Cannington to north of the river in Duncraig, and at the time, I was working in the inner northern suburbs of Osborne Park. I remember on one occasion, due to the commute, I stayed at the Rendezvous Scarborough Hotel on a Sunday night so I could get my eldest to school Monday morning. The commute made it easier for the boys to be with their mum during the week and with me on weekends. This experience certainly brought back memories of my absent father, which was not something I wanted for my boys. I wanted to be more present.

After a short while, a good friend rented his property to me. It was north of the river, about 20-minutes away from the kids' mum's house, and we stayed there for a couple of years. As the kids got older, various after-school and weekend activities started happening, and the juggle with the commute became more of a challenge. There were many situations where I would pick the kids up from school and we'd head to the shops or sit in the parked car to pass time before training started – there simply wasn't enough time to pick them up, head back home, and get back to sports. The boys weren't fans of this commute.

At this particular point in time, I had part-time custody of the kids, so taking time out from work was not really something I had to consider. Most employers back then were okay with you finishing one hour earlier once or twice a week to pick up kids etc., but that was the extent of flexibility in the workplace for men.

Eventually I found a rental just minutes from their mum's house, and in the same suburb as their school and sporting commitments.

Now that I was closer, even when they were with their mum, I could still spend time with them through their various sporting activities. To this day, I am actively involved with their sports clubs and assist during their training sessions when needed. I used to coach, but after one season, I quickly learned that I don't have the patience for it! I've even ventured into volunteering on the baseball club committee.

The biggest challenge I now face is finding an employer with the flexibility to allow me to work shortened hours during my week with the boys. When I started my own consulting business, the flexibility worked really well! The business was successful for about 18-months, but when it dried up, I struggled to find employment for about six months. While I certainly got the flexibility I wanted with my children, work stability became a real issue. Debts piled up, and the taxman cometh—in fact, he still cometh today! I immersed myself in all things my kids were doing to ignore what was happening on the outside. I was too proud to seek help or tell anyone. Financially, it took a toll, from which I am still recovering today.

Hello COVID-19.

Just before COVID, I found myself a new job with a registered training organisation. This job provided me with some flexibility through the pandemic and had a great business owner—my boss—who understood my situation. I was earning two-thirds less than previously, just managing to stay afloat, but flexibility for my kids was my priority.

Thanks to my new boss, a former Chief Financial Officer, who helped me work out some of my financial challenges and put me in touch with an accountant to guide me through my debt. If I can offer any advice to you, it's this: if you are in a financial pickle, put pride aside and seek help as soon as you can.

I met a wonderful primary school teacher who lived close to my sister. She loved how involved I was with my boys and encouraged me to seek out shared care. She had two boys of similar age, and our kids got on extremely well. Thankfully our parenting arrangements aligned thanks to my boys' mum accommodating the change.

About six months into this relationship, we hit a speed bump. My partner felt like she was no longer the priority and that my kids' sporting commitments were the priority. I was managing my kids' footy teams, coaching baseball, helping out at trainings, and—remembering I have two boys—going to all the games. Looking at it from an outsider's perspective, I really didn't have time for anyone else except for my kids.

I spoke to my sister, and she said the same thing. When I spoke to my mum, she also agreed. I was stunned. I had taken my oath of never being absent to an all-consuming level. I was sacrificing my wider family and my relationships without an appropriate balance.

When I look back, many parents and friends always commented on how engaged and active I was with my two boys.

I took the feedback from my partner, sister, and mum on board. Not long after, I sought out professional help, initially with a counsellor and then with a psychologist. I wanted to understand more about myself, how my relationship with my dad has affected me, and how it has all shaped the way I am now.

Based on some of these sessions and wanting to ensure my partner at the time felt like she was a priority, I started to pull back on how involved I was with my boys' sports. I did ask if my boys were disappointed, but they never indicated that they were. Unfortunately, after three years, that relationship ended.

For those of you navigating the world as a single father, seek feedback from those around you. Don't ignore it, investigate it. Hopefully it helps you improve and become a better father, partner, person. It's a great way to demonstrate to your kids that self-awareness and self-development is something worth learning.

While I was working with the training company, I was barely getting by financially. I earned enough to pay the bills, just. After two years, an opportunity came along to increase my earnings. Part of the negotiation during the interview was that, as a single father with two kids and limited support, I would require flexibility to do school runs every second week and would work additional hours in my week off to make up for any potential loss in productivity.

I started the new gig in the construction and mining industry at the beginning of the school holidays, just before Christmas. Shortly after starting, I ended up tearing my Achilles playing baseball and eventually underwent surgery and hospitalisation, twice. Not long after returning to work, I was terminated as I was not 'present' enough.

What I have found in my many years in that industry is that it is very much about being visible. Being seen in the office is seen to be doing something, not necessarily doing anything of value.

The later you stayed, the more kudos you gained. That was my experience, anyway.

Fortunately, my next role in the health sector was fully remote, as is my current role in the video games sector, allowing me to work from home. Both organisations empower and encourage employees to have a more balanced life. This flexibility reaps so many rewards.

Habits are heard to break.

I am now in what I consider to be the best job ever. Working in the video games sector, hiring people to make video games for Keywords Studios, working with like-minded people, and having full flexibility.

My kids are now back on the priority list—well, it's not as if they haven't been. I'm helping them out at training, playing baseball myself, and now on the baseball committee for the same club my kids and I play for. While life is very busy, I still need to ensure I take time out for me, and the scary world of mid-40s dating.

It's been a crazy 14 years as a father, mostly as a single one. There have been plenty of great times, and many challenging ones. Sometimes I wonder how I did—and do—manage it?!

If there's anything you take away from my chapter, I hope it's this: Don't let your pride get in the way of things. Be open and honest. Talk to people. Talk to your friends, family, and professionals. And don't forget to put yourself first, too. Doing what makes you happy will allow you to show up happier and be better for your family.

JOE BOVELL

> THIS I DO KNOW: HAVING CHILDREN IS, AND WILL BE, THE GREATEST ACHIEVEMENT IN MY LIFE. CAREER SUCCESS, SPORTING WINS, ENRICHING HOBBIES – NOTHING WILL EVER SURPASS THE HIGHS AND LOWS OF PARENTHOOD.

Joe is a 53-year-old father of two, a son aged 18 and a daughter aged 15. For over 30 years, Joe has built a diverse and enriching career in a variety of roles ranging from banking, a trade in horticulture, owning an ad agency, and now the CEO and Managing Director of a national manufacturing company in the agribusiness sector.

JOE BOVELL

AUTHOR NAME: JOE BOVELL
BUSINESS NAME: ECO GROWTH
POSITION: CEO AND MANAGING DIRECTOR
BUSINESS INDUSTRY: AGRIBUSINESS/MANUFACTURING
WEBSITE: WWW.ECOGROWTH.COM.AU
LINKEDIN: LINKEDIN.COM/IN/JOE-BOVELL-65083620

AN INTRODUCTION TO ME

My first days on this earth started with hardship, unimaginable stress, and pain, but I was none the wiser.

It was July 1970, my mother was just 17 years and one month old. As I came screaming into this world on a cold winter's day, my birth signified an arrival that society was still not ready to embrace: single motherhood. My father had no interest in seeing me, ever. Shamefully, neither did my maternal grandparents, who took the decision to evict my mother onto the streets of Perth with a one-day-old baby in hand.

Nowhere to go, no money, no resources.

It was just us and one suitcase with hand-me-downs gifted from King Edward Hospital. The first two nights of my existence, we stayed in a police lockup; the next few, a nun's convent. Where else to go when you don't know what to do? Help was limited.

My journey to being the father I am today is unconventional, but perhaps not unique.

I've never met my father, and with no male role model in my

childhood, I became the 'man of the house' at a very young age. I grew up before my time. I had no mentor, no benchmark, no sounding board. I had to figure out a lot of the 'male stuff' on my own, a tough task given I grew up pre-internet; unfortunately, I couldn't just Google the answers to my many—and complex— questions. I was parented by a single mother who fulfilled both parental roles (I swear she disciplined for three, though!).

I am going to be brutally honest in this chapter. It may be uncomfortable at times for the reader, and I apologise in advance. Perhaps you can find solace in the fact that, while it was a little uncomfortable for me to write, I did so with the hope that you might take away the idea that being committed to having a positive family environment can be the conduit to healing the trauma of the past.

My storyline is that perseverance, resilience, and a strong focus on creating a better future led me to where I am today and to the father I wanted to be. TW: domestic violence and abuse.

CHILDHOOD AND ITS IMPACT ON WORK ETHIC

My childhood could best be described as anything but ideal; it was traumatic and life-changing. My mother did the best she could, but I experienced pain and hurt that no child ever should. I saw things that can't be unseen: domestic violence, alcoholism, and sexual abuse alongside other traumatic and unmentionable events.

But through it all, I survived. Resilient and driven, determined to break the vicious cycle, to not repeat the sins of others.

A sad tale, but nonetheless, the childhood I experienced inevitably helped shape me into the father I am today.

My upbringing not only shaped my overall approach to how I wanted to live my life, but it also certainly had a significant impact on my work ethic and desire to self-improve.

We lived below the poverty line – from pension cheque to pension cheque. Second hand clothes, basic food, no luxuries, no holidays, no fashionable labels. Kmart was as good as it got, and back in the '70s, it wasn't as trendy as it is today! Can you imagine a 17-year-old woman dealing with that level of adversity some 53 years ago? Seeking charity, a handout, and a hand up, bereft of hope, all the while dealing with societal pressures and prejudice. Thankfully, there are far greater resources available to those in need today, but there's still so much more to be done.

My mother is an amazing woman who displayed courage and resilience in the face of adversity not experienced by many in their lifetime.

If I wanted something, I had to go and earn it. And that's exactly what I did. I started casual work at the ripe old age of 10, selling newspapers for 4c each. I worked all week for less than $10, but to a kid with no money, that was a lot, especially one who liked lollies and toys.

I haven't been a day out of work since.

My career has been based on hard work, luck, a preparedness to take on challenges, and, above all else, a fierce will to never give in or give up. To be a better version than what I was last year, an upgrade of sorts. It's a gift and a burden. It certainly hasn't been linear, but I'm comfortable with where it's ended up thus far.

FATHERHOOD INSECURITIES AND LESSONS LEARNED
Just before my first child was born, I had enormous reservations. I was nervous, anxious, and insecure. These feelings were so deep and ingrained that I didn't share them with anyone, including my wife. My greatest fear was by not having a father in my life, would that negatively impact the dad I wanted to be?

I took the stance that while I may not know what I was doing, I would do whatever I could to create an environment that fostered the best possible childhood for my kids—one that was safe, loving, and nurturing. I was very fortunate in that my wife shared the same ethos, so we were both on the same page from the very beginning.

Like most dads, I want what's best for my children. I want them to be successful, happy, healthy, to achieve their full potential, and above all else, be good human beings.

I am not the perfect father, far from it, and I'm sure my two teenage children would testify to that fact. What I do know is that I am continually learning to be a better dad. And just when I think I've nailed it, I get a sharp reminder that I still have a long way to go.

This I do know: having children is, and will be, the greatest achievement in my life. Career success, sporting wins, enriching hobbies – nothing will ever surpass the highs and lows of parenthood. It's the best job in the world, but also the toughest.

MY MANTRAS

My commitment as a father has been based on the following mantras:

To protect my children. I will do whatever I can to never let them suffer the way I did.

To have a safe and secure upbringing. A stable home life.

To not have them worry about where the next dollar is coming from, to not have to go without.

To pass on my knowledge and experiences so they can learn from my mistakes in the hope I can help forge their pathway to success.

To educate and guide them so they can then pass that onto future generations.

To be the best father I can possibly be while recognising I have my faults and I won't be perfect.

While I never sought out my biological father, I do, at times, wonder why he chose not to experience the joy I have had in being a present and committed father. Only he can answer that. They say you don't miss what you don't have, but creating Father's Day cards in primary school was never an enjoyable experience for me.

The upside to my loss (and his) was that it gave me great resolve to be as involved as humanly possible in my children's lives.

Sporting events, assemblies, school excursions—you name it, I tried to get to all of them. To be present. To be 'Father of the Year.'

Naturally I couldn't get to every event. Work does get in the way sometimes, but I did attend more than the average dad would.

Continuing on the path of brutal honesty, it's important for me to discuss the profound effect my upbringing has had on me as a man and a parent. I mentioned earlier that the adversity faced in my youth has been both a gift and a burden.

It has given me a drive and purpose that can't be easily obtained or found in the majority of the population. It has made me appreciate the simple things in life, along with the finer ones! I never take for granted a hotel stay, a restaurant dinner, or an interstate flight. I believe it has prevented the development of any hubris, keeping me grounded and always aware of where I have come from.

On the other hand, I'm never satisfied or comfortable, scared I might end up back below the poverty line. The reality of that happening is of course unlikely, especially now that I'm in my 50s. But in my mind, it's still a possibility. I can't fully relax or appreciate what I have achieved, fearing that spending too long looking in the rear-view mirror might take my eye off the ball.

I have always wanted my kids to have what I didn't. I am proud to say they haven't suffered, gone without, and have had privileged and fortunate lives thus far. But it's been far from perfect.

Unfortunately, my relationship with my children has been negatively impacted by my desire to instil unbreakable resilience in them. I wanted them to understand the value of a dollar, the importance of hard work, and the reality that life might not always be easy. My fault lies in pushing too hard, aiming for the best for them but not necessarily delivering it with a silver spoon. I haven't savoured the moment enough, always focused on their future and not the present. In recent times, I've come to realise that this wasn't the right approach.

There is no instruction manual for parenting. Yes, there is the internet that provides a multitude of differing opinions for every situation, but you soon realise that not everything applies to your family, and only causes confusion and angst for all concerned. You learn on the spot, observing, and listening to others.

You try your utmost best to be the best father you can be, and then one day, you get told by your teenage children how you could have fulfilled your duties better. Children can be brutal in their feedback, and I can assure you it's difficult to hear when your whole life has been centred around providing and protecting them. Families tend to be far more honest with you than your work colleagues will ever be. It's important to balance that feedback, however, with the vagaries of teenagerhood!

I feel I did the best I could as a father but have now come to realise I could have done better. I wish I invested more into my own well-being to allow me to move on from my past so I could have a level of freedom in the present. This would have facilitated a different environment for my family. It wasn't toxic, but it could have been healthier.

I have sought professional help for my own sake and that of those close to me. It has given me a greater appreciation for the importance of good mental health and not feeling ashamed to seek help when needed. My biases have shifted considerably away from the stereotypical male perception of weakness to that of considerable strength and courage in seeking help. I see that as an invaluable, firsthand experience that money can't buy – not only to be a better father but also as a leader professionally.

WORK AND FATHERHOOD

I didn't take parental leave and fortunately my wife was a stay-at-home mum. Our children never went to daycare – this was simply a parenting decision we made early on.

I've been fortunate to have had jobs whereby either I had a degree of flexibility, or I simply deprioritised my work and personal life to prioritise my family. I've always thought that the work/life balance is a fallacy – and it pretty much is. The conundrum we all face is we need to provide for our families, so work must take priority. While that's stating the obvious, what's not so clear is what we can do to manage our priority list effectively, ensuring we can make the important moments count. The moral of the story is that I made family so important to me that my employer recognised that.

Perspective is a compelling catalyst for change. My previous employers didn't value family and/or me as a human being. I had little regard for them and left of my own volition.

I've seen companies with employees who gave 10-plus years of service be disrespected and dispatched without consideration of their emotional and financial well-being. A number not a person. The reality is, some people work to live, and others live to work. Not everyone loves their job, and those who do are very lucky indeed.

I am the CEO and Managing Director of a national manufacturing company supplying fertiliser to the agribusiness sector. Eco Growth in many ways is a disrupter, taking on the traditional players, punching above its weight, and trying to succeed in an industry that is typically low margin, high volume, and high risk. I thrive on that challenge, the underdog of sorts fighting the 500-pound gorillas. Our business is built on the back of a fantastic product and great people. It's difficult to have one without the other.

My position means from time to time, I have to make tough decisions, generally about people. I've had to condition myself to have the difficult conversations. Typically, they are about not adhering to the standards we want as a business. More often than not, it's about their behaviour more so than their work performance. It doesn't always end well but I will always default to being a decent human being and work with people first to help them address any issues at hand and improve.

The relationship is not always mutually beneficial, but when all is said and done, we spend so much of our lives at work that if it's not a two-way street, it has to be asked: Are you working for the right people, and conversely, do you have the right people working for you?

I challenge you to have that conversation with yourself. If you have an employer that 'walks the walk' in regards to family first, then they should be supportive of that approach.

As a CEO, I adhere to the 'family first' mantra. My ethos is simple: go to the school assembly, attend the sports day, look after your children when they are sick, and don't fret about being 10-minutes late for work because you had trouble getting them in the car to go to school.

You never get those moments back. Once they are gone, they are gone forever.

When travelling for work, technology has fortunately made missing those moments a little more palatable. Being able to Face-Time with your kids has been transformative for me and many others. Young children can't understand why dad has gone away and what he is doing while he's there. If they can see your face, your hotel room, your workplace, they gain a much greater understanding, which helps to de-stress the situation. Time differences when travelling domestically can work to your advantage, and I try to make the most of that, particularly during the witching hour. Your partner will also thank you for it!

As my kids have grown older, the ability to text, email, or interact on social media helps fill that void. Now they are so used to me travelling that when I return home, I inevitably get asked, "Did you go away?" It's nice not to be missed!

I made the decision a long time ago not to go through life bitter and twisted, not to blame my non-existent father, but to appreciate what I had as a child rather than what I didn't. In fact, I laugh now at the thought of Kmart shoes and bowl haircuts. It made me who I am today. The good and the bad. Warts and all.

I have my faults, but I think overall the good outweighs the bad. As a man and as a father.

I live and breathe the ethos that no matter how high up the

ladder you climb or how important you believe you are (generally, you are not), you should be grounded in everything that you do. Treat people with kindness, show empathy, be ethical, and understand that your people, staff, and stakeholders have lives outside of the workplace that are generally far more important than inside it. Above all else, default to being a good human being and help others to be just that.

I have learned many lessons in my life, but perhaps the most salient is this: I regret the things I didn't do rather than the things I did.

ABOUT SARAH MACONACHIE

WWW.WORKHARDPARENTHARD.COM.AU

Sarah can be described as determined, tenacious, and driven to achieve her goals. From a young age, Sarah had a big vision and significant life goals, as well as a fire in her belly to ensure she always achieved what she set out to do. With her optimistic nature, she has always believed that things will work out, and with an ethos that everything happens for a reason, she believes her life has unfolded just as it was meant to.

Originally from the UK, Sarah graduated with a degree in Psychology and soon decided she wanted to embark on an adventure exploring the world, refusing to settle in a place that didn't feel right. She booked a one-way ticket to Australia and never looked back.

Living in Sydney, Australia, Sarah embarked on a career in Human Resources and Recruitment. When Sarah and her husband decided to move to Perth to start a family and be closer to her husband's family, the world delivered once again. Just a week after her husband was offered a job in Perth, Sarah found out she was expecting her first baby, and her motherhood journey began.

Since returning to work after having children, Sarah recognised the need to "bridge the gap" and create more equality for mothers in the workforce. Sarah hears more and more from women that have taken huge pay cuts, have been demoted, and have had to take junior positions once they become mothers. This bias, whether conscious or subconscious, has fed into societal norms from days gone by that once women become mothers, that is their only role in society.

The feeling that we must sacrifice money or seniority to have the flexibility to be a mother also leaves women feeling unstimulated, lacking in confidence, and with low self-worth. There are women who would love to get back to work but struggle to understand how they could possibly balance their new life of having dependents and a career.

On the other hand, men in the workforce are being told they cannot work flexible hours, facing challenges in balancing their career and supporting their family at home. They fear potential setbacks in promotions and bonuses if they choose to utilise their parental leave or take time off to be with their children.

Sarah's own journey led her to write for various publications on topics related to parenthood, working parents, gender equity, and mindset. Her interest and research have resulted in publications challenging the status quo for working parents, presenting perspectives from both mothers and fathers. This inspiration prompted her to write 'Working Mothers Inspiring Others' and 'Working Dads and Balancing Acts'. The aim of both these books is to normalise the need for balance for parents with careers, to share the mental load of parenting, and to provide support and encouragement to mothers who want to re-enter the workforce.

Sarah's desire to support parents through the transition of parenthood is the driving force behind all her endeavours related to parenting, including her own business, Work Hard Parent Hard.

CONCLUSION

As we close the inspirational chapters our dads have shared, I invite you to take a moment to reflect on your own experience as a father. Are you satisfied with the balance you have between work and home? What did you relate to? What inspired you? What do you want to incorporate into your own life?

Dads are no longer seen as just the sole provider of the household. More and more dads want the flexibility to do school pick-ups or drop-offs, spend days at home with their young ones, take their kids to sporting events, and make the intentional decision to be present.

As more women want to return to work, the parental responsibilities are now being shared more equally than ever before. This shift across society is not only incredible for the development of our children, but it also creates a healthy balance within the household, whatever the working arrangements.

Our children are a reflection of us. They are born with a blank slate, and the way they think and behave is shaped by their parents and the environment they are brought up in. Creating a life you love, being passionate about what you do, and being present with your family is essential for the happiness of you and your children.

Use the worksheets in this book to reflect on what you really want in life. How can you create the work/life balance that you truly want? Are you happy at work? Do you feel passionate about your chosen career? Are you satisfied with the time you spend with your children, or could you do more?

We have control over our own lives, so it's up to you to create the life that you love.

REFLECTION

- What was your biggest take away from the Chapters

_____

_____

_____

_____

_____

_____

_____

_____

_____

_____

- Name one thing you are going to implement that you learnt from the Chapters

_____

_____

_____

_____

- How do you feel about your own balance of working and being a parent?

_____

_____

_____

_____

_____

_____

_____

_____

_____

YOUR PURPOSE

When we have children we go through a huge process of change. Pre children we have a carefree life, a job, time to ourselves, no real commitments. We can do what we want, when we want to.

When we have children our perspectives and priorities make an incredible shift. Our children become our priority and we go through a process of figuring out what our purpose is now, what we want and need in order to make us happy and our children/ family happy.

I want you to think about the following questions, and answer them as truthfully as you can.

- Do you enjoy staying home with your children full time or Part time?
- Do you enjoy working?
- Do you feel you need a balance of working and being home with your children? What would that look like?
- When do you have time for yourself? and do you actively book things in for you?
- Are you passionate about what you do?

These questions are so important to think about. We often feel like we have to sacrifice something especially in the early years of being a parent, but compromising on the different areas of your life is a much way to look at it.

Being happy makes for much happier children. So it's time to focus on YOU and what your purpose is, what do you want?

Rate the following areas of your life out of 10 and see where you are compromising on and if you are happy with that.

- Work/ Career
- Parenting
- Social Life
- Relationship
- Time for self
- Holidays/ Travel

HAVE A CLEAR VISION OF WHAT YOU REALLY WANT AND SET A CLEAR GOAL!

Totally relax and let your imagination wonder. Take some time to close your eyes and let your imagination wonder. Think about your life over the next 12 months. If you had all the resources, time, money and support to live exactly how you want to- what would that look like?

Think about all the different areas of your life. What kind of house do you live in, holidays/ travel, education, relationships, business/career, your finances. Allow your imagination to build a beautiful picture of your ideal life in your mind. Your imagination is your real self- make sure it's what you would really love.

Write down a shopping list of your personal and professional wants as if they are in the present tense.

Write down a list of your personal and professional wants

_____

_____

_____

_____

_____

_____

_____

_____

_____

_____

_____

THINK ABOUT YOUR BELIEFS- THIS IS WHAT YOU ARE TEACHING YOUR CHILDREN EVEN IF YOU DON'T KNOW IT!

FINANCIAL WEALTH

If your income was to stop tomorrow, how long could you sustain your lifestyle?

What is the most you have earned in a 12 month period?

How much would you need to earn to consider yourself wealthy?

BUSINESS/ CAREER

When you wake up in the morning, do you feel excited about what you do?

If you could do anything in your career, what would it be?

HOLIDAYS

How often do you go on holiday? Where do you go? What type of accommodation do you stay in? Are you able to do what you want freely?

HOME

How would you describe the house you live in? Is it in an area you love?

RELATIONSHIPS

How would you describe your relationships with your family and friends?

CHILDREN

Are you happy with the amount of time you spend with your children?

Are their any aspects of your own upbringing that you would like to change in the upbringing of your own children?

Do you understand why your children think and behave the way they do?

How you answered those questions gives a very clear indication of where your paradigms sit. It should have made you think about where you are now, and where you would love to be.

How we think and behave also has a direct reflection on how you are raising your children to think and behave,

When you answered the questions, think about if you want to change, what is the life that you truly want to live?

How do you want your children to be raised to think and behave?

WORK HARD PARENT HARD DAILY SUCCESS GUIDE

1. **Morning Dream Session:** Before you even think about escaping the clutches of your oh-so-comfy bed, keep those peepers shut! Picture your dream life. You know, the one where you're not just scraping Weetabix off the kitchen table but living large and in charge! Feel it – the pride, the joy, the "I've-got-my-life-together" vibes.

2. **Gratitude Graffiti:** Now, hop out of bed and jot down 10 things that make you feel grateful. It could be your kiddo's toothless grin, your partner finally remembering to put the toilet seat down, or just the fact that coffee exists. Close your eyes, take a deep breath, and send some cosmic high-fives to the universe. Got someone bugging you? Imagine texting them, "Hey, you're awesome, and I am so grateful you have stopped using my mug."

3. **Ideal You:** Write down your "worthy ideal." Something like, "I'm over the moon that I've finally mastered the art of hiding veggies in meals so my kids eat them." Keep telling yourself this – your subconscious is listening (and it's a better listener than your toddler).

4. **Self Pep-Talk:** Time for your daily affirmation. Try: "I'm an excellent parent. I am great in my career, I spend quality time with my children, and I have the balance of both down pat."

5. **Life Script:** This is your chance to be the scriptwriter of your own blockbuster life. "I always have enough money to buy whatever I want for myself and my family "

6. **Action Hero Mode:** Write down 6 things you will do today. They need to be action points that will help you to reach our overall goal, if it's something someone else could do- remove it from the list immediately!

7. **Priority Juggling:** Throughout the day, tackle things based on how much they'll help you reach your "Goal." Got a problem? Take a deep breath, channel your inner Zen master, and ask, "What would Super Me do?"

8. **Goal Card Gala:** Whip your goal card whenever possible. It's like a backstage pass to your dreams.

9. **Worthy Ideal Check:** Whatever you're doing – conquering the world or just staring into space – ask yourself, "Is this getting me closer to my dream?"

10. **Nighty-Night Manifestation:** Repeat your morning dream session before you hit the hay. The mood you snooze in sets the tone for your morning!

REMEMBER: You are what you think about. Choose those thoughts like you choose your battles – wisely and with a sense of humour! The great thing is you can do all of these while spending time with your little ones. I ask my 4 year old what she is grateful for most days and it's always a beautiful response!